TRUTH
RESTORED

Dear Reader,

Catching a glimpse of our potential as human beings shows us the world as an infinite realm filled with passion; one filled with possibilities. We are not born courageous, nor are we born with ambition, and our qualities are not prescribed. But one thing is for sure: our infinite potential begins before we take our first breath, and its radiance is sustained *only* until we breathe our last. For this reason, I refuse to wait any longer. With falsehood's propagation, I cannot tolerate the corruption it causes, and especially so in the Muslim community. Certainly, the vicious attempt to destroy Islam is alarming, but worse to me are those who shroud their hypocrisy under the umbrella of this beautiful religion. The truth is urging to be declared, published, and upheld. To do so, I realized that the foundation needs to be resurfaced from under the rubles of distortion... and so **TRUTH RESTORED** was born.

I decided to keep my identity secret – going by the pseudonym **SACREDLIGHT** – for the simple reason that I want my full reward in an infinite world. Some will stand before God, on the day of judgement, not worthy of the reward of the afterlife for having already received the benefits of their deed in this finite world. I do not want to be that person. Nonetheless, I wrote this book with passion; I wrote it with love. And I hope that you will enjoy reading it as much as I did writing it.

Sincerely,

TRUTH RESTORED

Uncoiling the twists of truth...

In a world filled with falsehood.

By SACREDLIGHT

Ordering Information:
Look for TRUTH RESTORED – By SACREDLIGHT – on www.amazon.com

ISBN 978-0-692-97951-8
Library of Congress Number is available
Printed in the United States of America

First Edition

To our beloved awaited one.

Author's Preface

Imagine the human mental development since birth, the intricate assimilation of developmental values, and the subjective acquisition of knowledge. Imagine, if you will, the labyrinthine realm of curiosity, the strong desire to discover, and the search for ideals. Imagine... the human intellect. It sets goals for itself that no programmer has prepared or initiated. It holds on to the contemplative complexities that render it happy, sad, or maybe even something in-between. It strives for wisdom, moral judgment, and ultimately, peace.

These personal conditions – the most precious aspects of the human mind – made me ponder upon what *the truth* really is. The subject haunted my daily thoughts, and at night invaded my dreams. It will seem that, by all means, the truth is true. When seeking it, however, I realized the extent to which my five senses could betray me. *I could be deaf to the truth,* I thought to myself, *and perhaps could not even feel, taste, nor smell what is real, and could definitely be blind if I took **only** what seems obvious into consideration.* Why? Because we are human beings. Beyond what our senses perceive lies what may never be conceived, unless our internal inhibitions are alleviated, and our cognitive process allowed to soar above the highest clouds of our mind. Only then, are we able to see the truth in its pristine, unaltered, untainted beauty. From high above our cognitive clouds, far from perturbation and falsehood, it becomes easy to discern that the religion of Islam is the absolute truth.

And as human beings, we have been given the privilege to exist, as well as the instinctive will to succeed. However, success is not the destination, but the trip toward it. Are not the happiest moments of our lives when we are traveling toward a worthy ideal? Earl Nightingale puts it beautifully. He says:

"Success is the progressive realization of a worthy ideal."

I closed my eyes and found Islam; a religion that gives us the utmost worthiness: *love*. Without it, we would not know our purpose, and life would be as if traveling very fast… nowhere. But, upon opening my eyes, I saw distort hindering the natural process of Islam's beautiful system. I saw treachery and deceit tainting its legitimate elegance and, upon further investigation, I found a fingerprint. A well-known entity had been hard at work to dismantle the essential flow of human reasoning. Using my trusty pen, I decided to fight back; I decided to write.

I have always yearned for an all-encompassing book containing reference to the basic foundation of the truth, upon which further knowledge can be built. A publication that recovers the bedrock of truth, i.e., its true source containing untainted purity. The aim is to straighten, make tidy, and rectify the bending of the truth in order to analyze, formulate, interpret, confirm, define, and clarify in pursuance of exposing and eradicating falsehood. You hold this book in the palm of your hands. How do I know the truth myself, you ask? Well, I have the privilege to be acquainted with its representatives, its protectors, its ambassadors.

Read on... I will introduce you.

"And say, truth has come and falsehood has departed. Indeed, falsehood is always departing." – **Qur'an 17:81**

This is also to you

For alleviating pain, when confronting falsehood weighed on me

For soothing, when I was perplexed as the world puzzled me

For sharing and caring, when the nights were long

For ardor and passion, thus keeping me strong

This is also to you... my best friend: My wife.

TABLE OF CONTENTS

~ PART ONE ~

BEYOND THE OBVIOUS

I was blind with eyes wide open. Now that they are shut... I can see clearly.

There are countless books that focus on a specific subject, dissecting it piece by piece and shedding light on categorical information. This is not one of them. TRUTH RESTORED contains a secret that is not directly seen, nor heard, nor touched, but only felt. One that is not usurped by eyes or ears, but invited by the heart. I believe that this secret surprises, intrigues, and fascinates. And I hope that by the end of the book you would have experienced these feelings from the broad brush strokes it paints.

If you are a non-Muslim, prepare to understand, ponder, and love. If you are a Muslim, prepare to see Islam from an elite perspective. And although some sections will contain familiar information, do not skip them, because a reminder benefits the believers. When the last page has turned, the absolute truth will be revealed.

The flow of the book is in such a way that anyone can benefit from the information contained herein. In the end it all makes sense, and the basic foundation of Truth is recovered thanks to all that came before.

In this first part, we will close our eyes and see the strangers that we are. But forget I said that... and allow me into your heart.

"So have they not traveled the earth and have hearts with which to reason and ears with which to hear? For, indeed, it is not eyes that are blinded, but blinded are the hearts which are within the bosom."

– Qur'an 22:46

Chapter 1
SYNAPTIC TRUTH

In the world we inhabit, we are strangers. In our psyche, many things are not as they seem. We sometimes create for ourselves personalized thoughts which turn into realities; strangers in a realm that we have shaped and fashioned. We belong to a world in which everything is relative, and view our existence through a typified lens. When blemished, this lens renders our experiences either blurry or distorted as a result. Do we see with our eyes, or are they mere messengers? Do we hear with our ears, or are they simply the medium? Are our senses the temple of veracity, or are they only the faculty through which impressions are conveyed? In reality, what we see, smell, feel, hear, and taste – in its raw form – could very well *not* be an accurate representation of the world. Our senses do not provide us with direct access, but only send signals to our brain which then processes and interprets. Our eyes, for example, are not *mere windows* to the world outside. The images we see are our personalized version of the world. For instance, we sometimes look at something and, for a fraction of a second, see something completely different. Why does that happen? Where does the *other* perception come from? Well, we create our reality in our *self*, based on interpretations of our brain, and perceive the world according to our pre-existing tendencies. Relying on our genetic blueprint, which is further modified by experience, we assume how the world is. This assumption affects, to some extent, even our physiology. To further reinforce this fact, I will ask you a simple question: Is there any interpretation mechanism that exists within the structures of the eye? Let us see...

The eye has a very interesting design allowing visual information to be collected and processed by several entities that, although intricate as a group, actually have simple functions on their own. The eye's main structures are the cornea, the iris, the pupil, the retina, and the optic nerve, and they all work in tandem to **only** capture, translate, and forward the information to the brain. Nothing more. The cornea is simply a rigid transparent structure covering the front of the eye. In addition to protecting delicate entities, it focuses incoming light onto the retina. The iris is a heavily pigmented muscle group, which dilates and constricts the pupil to regulate the amount of light entering. The pupil is a hole in the iris, allowing light to fall upon the retina which is, in turn, composed of multiple layers of cells lining the inside of the eyeball. These layers work together to translate light patterns into information the brain can use. Finally, the optic nerve is a bundle of nerve fibers that carries the visual information from the eye to the brain. This bundle of nerves is located in what is known as the optic disc; the portion of the retina where these nerves and blood vessels pass through the back of the eye. This disc is also known as the blind spot because it contains no photoreceptors. Consequently, all the visual information these structures gather and transmit is actually processed in the brain. Thus, we do not *see* with our eyes, and must look *within* for assessment of any value. The images you see are neither beautiful nor ugly. They are... *your perspective.*

Interestingly enough, our other senses operate similarly, in that they also send the message to the brain for interpretation. Our sensory inputs need to be interpreted because our nervous system, of which the brain is a member, communicates using electrical signals. The brain processes information via *neurotransmitters* sent from one *neuron* to another. Neurons are brain cells. They are the core of our being, and operate in a matter that is fascinating. They are to human beings what electricity is to computers. It is through these intriguing cells that we essentially exist and interact; they are who we are.

The Neuron

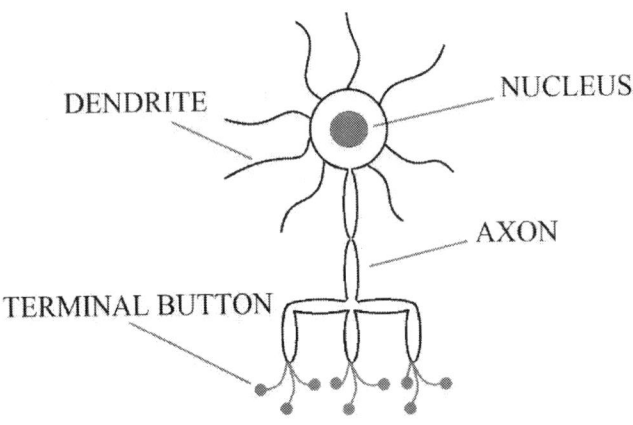

Approximately one hundred billion neurons are found throughout a normal adult's nervous system. They are similar to other cells found throughout the rest of the body; in that they are surrounded by a membrane and have a nucleus which contains genes. Neurons, like other cells, also contain *cytoplasm* and *mitochondria*, as well as other organelles. However, they differ in that they have specialized extended branches called *dendrites* and *axons*. Dendrites bring information into the neuron, and axons send information away to the next one. These cells communicate with each other through an electrochemical process: neurotransmitters are sent from the terminal buttons of the first neuron to the dendrites of the next. This medium, known as a *synapse*, takes place in a gap between any two neurons communicating with each other, and these electrical signals are known as *action potential*. I have always been fascinated by the fact that anything the brain does is achieved via synaptic transmission; viz. *electricity*.

The Synapse

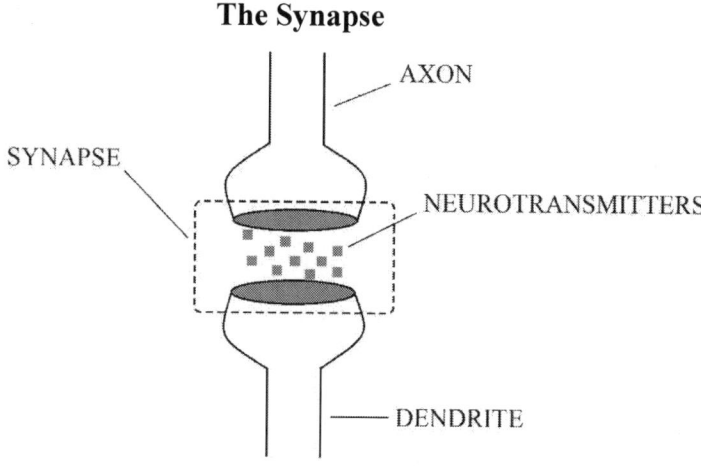

A newborn possesses a number of neurons which stop reproducing after infancy. On the other hand, dendrites, axons, as well as the interconnectivity between neurons, increase throughout life; they spread as long as stimuli exist. A pattern of synapses is drawn between neural networks every time we learn something new. As such, if you learn to rollerblade at seven years old and stop for twenty years, the exercise will still feel somewhat familiar even if this large gap of time exists. It sure became weak, and you might wobble a little because you were not practicing, but you would still be able to rollerblade because the synaptic pattern drawn between your neurons when you were seven is still there twenty years later.

The same thing happens every time we learn something new, i.e., patterns of synaptic circuitry are constantly initiated. Further, the more we practice a particular skill, the stronger our synapses become. When asked about how they are so good at what they do, all athletes have answered saying that they constantly practice – over and over, and over again. They even sometimes, with their eyes shut, imagine themselves practicing. Hence, *"practice makes perfect"*. Of course, other factors also play a role. *Glial cells*, for example, another kind of cell that acts like glue, strengthen the synaptic process. But the underlying concept is the same: the more we do something, the better we become at it until it eventually even becomes an extension of ourselves. Worship and prayer also initiate synaptic circuitry in the brain, and these impulses end up defining the architecture of thoughts and inclinations. But I am getting ahead of myself...

Because the brain is where the world is interpreted, all peripheral input received through several forms of energy (kinetic, chemical, light, and sound) have to be converted into electrical signals in order for the brain to process the information. This process, known as transduction, is best portrayed by our sense of hearing. Our ears are extraordinary organs. They not only receive the sounds around us, but also translate this information into the electrical impulses that our brain will understand. What I find truly exceptional is that the process is almost entirely mechanical. While our other senses rely on chemical and neurological reactions, our hearing physiology is based, to some extent, solely on physical movement. To start, sound is the sum of vibrations that travel through matter, and comes from air particles pushed by these vibrations. This creates a wave originating from the source of the sound, pushing air particles around the initial air particles, which consecutively push the air particles around them, and so on and so forth until the pulse reaches one of our ears, or both. This process is similar to ripples in the water. If you drop a stone in still water, the impact will cause ripples pushing each other away in all unrestricted directions, starting from where the stone initially landed. As another example, when a gong is struck, its matter (metal, wood, or plastic) will lean in and out with rapid successions. When flexing out on either side, it pushes the surrounding air particles, which then push the particles surrounding them, pushing the particles surrounding them, and so on until they reach the structures of our ears; namely: the pinna, the ear canal, the tympanic membrane, the ossicular chain (the hammer, the anvil, and the stirrup), the cochlea, the sensory cells, and the hearing nerve. The pinna is the outer part of our ear; protruding from our head. It is pointed forward and has many curves for a very interesting reason. Since sound bounces off the pinna, its designed curvatures give our brain the necessary details to include in its interpretation a sense of orientation. Thus, we understand where the sound is coming from.

Sound is then directed through the ear canal, at which end it reaches the tympanic membrane (a.k.a. the ear drum). This membrane is a thin and rigid piece of skin that sets the ossicular chain in motion, and the slightest change in air-pressure will make it vibrate. The ossicular chain consists of the hammer, the anvil, and the stirrup; a group of tiny little bones that create an interesting chain of events: the hammer pushes the stirrup, which sequentially moves the anvil. This intricate mechanical design transmits sound vibrations into the inner ear, within which lies a fascinating feature: the cochlea. The cochlea is a simple, spiral shaped, fluid filled body that almost looks like a seashell, which has a very complicated function: to translate the mechanical energy of sound into complex electrical signals. It is a tube filled with fluid and sensory cells (a.k.a. hair cells), which are instilled with varying degrees of sensitivity for the disclosure of varying frequencies, i.e., our ability to distinguish between the different tones of sound. To give you a sense of the fascinating complexity of this process, think about the fact that it is the movement of the fluid which sets in motion the hair cells in the cochlea, transforming mechanical energy into electrical impulses. As such is the final stage: the movement of the fluid in the cochlea causes tensions to be applied on the hair cells which, in turn, produce electrical signals that are transmitted to the brain via the hearing nerve. The auditory cortex of the brain receives these impulses and interprets them. Hence, we do not *hear* with our ears either.

Furthermore, not only do we not see with our eyes, nor hear with our ears, but we also do not feel with our skin, nor taste with our tongue. In fact, as funny as this might seem, we also even *smell* with our brain. Indeed, although the sense of smell starts with odor molecules that reach our nose and involve the nasal cavity mucus, the olfactory epithelium, receptor neurons, and the olfactory tract, the brain is where it ultimately *happens*. It all starts when molecules in the air are sniffed into our nostrils. Most of our immediate nasal cavity past that point is filled with sticky mucus that filters the air entering, trapping foreign materials that might damage our lungs. In our nasal cavity, we find the olfactory epithelium. This area houses special neurons which intercept the odor molecules that have gotten stuck on the mucus, and send the gathered data via signals transported through the olfactory tract to our brain. This information is relayed to several areas of the brain for interpretation. Only then, this process becomes perceived as the odor of whatever the initial molecules originated from. And there you have it; we also do not smell with our nose.

Although the speed of these processes is nothing short of amazing, with some nerve impulses traveling as fast as 120 miles per second, everything we experience happens one-tenth of a second before the brain actually interprets it. This short delay in recognition is due to the massive supply of information received. In light of this, the surprising quickness of brain functions is truly wondrous. In fact, the more I analyzed the human brain, the more I felt a sense of awe and reverence. But there was something even more fascinating… Although the brain is where it all physiologically happens, it is the mysterious unseen entity we call *the mind* that is ultimately the interpreter. In my humble opinion, our heart is conclusively involved – as the hardware. Not that we *think* with our hearts, but that it is ultimately the birthplace of wisdom and intuition.

"So have they not traveled through the earth and have hearts with which to reason…" – **Qur'an 22:46**

"In that is a reminder for whoever has a heart…" – **Qur'an 50:37**

"…He [God] *blames you for what your hearts have gained…"*
– Qur'an 2:225

But what of the difference between the brain and the mind? After all, the words *brain* and *mind* are often used interchangeably, and many a time even mistaken for one another. Well, they are in fact two very different entities in terms of corporeality. You see, the myth of *"we use only 10% of our brain,"* for instance, is just that; a myth. A more accurate statement would be: *we use only 10% of the potential of our mind.* The brain is a tangible organ that we actually use 100% of. It can be seen, touched, and resides in our skull for protection. Divided into parts (the brainstem, cerebellum, and cerebrum), the brain is the most complex organ of the human body. The cerebrum is further divided into lobes; namely, frontal, parietal, temporal, and occipital. These sections are all encompassed in two hemispheres connected by the *corpus callosum*; a string of nerve fibers located beneath the cerebral cortex, which transmits information back and forth between both hemispheres. The left brain hemisphere receives input from the right side of the body, and the right brain hemisphere receives input from the left side of the body. This process, known as *contralateral conduction*, gives us a glance into the complex management that the brain is responsible for, and the complexity of its operations continues to render the brain as an unsolved mystery – albeit limited. What is infinite, however, is the mind, for which exists another set of convolutions which also continues to baffle psychologists. For example, as I contemplate what to write next in this paragraph, what part of me is doing the contemplation? And if the scope of this subject was not beyond that of this book, I would have elaborated. But for the sake of being concise, I will instead elaborate on that which gives us a little glimpse into human cognition.

* ~ * ~ * ~ * ~ * ~ * ~ * ~ * ~ *

Have you ever asked yourself where subtle insights and sudden creative ideas come from? It seems as though as soon as space is available in our mind, imagination moves in to build the foundations of thought. But **where does** imagination come from, and how does it erect the monuments of reflection? These questions could be answered by inspecting an area that is usually neglected in our societies today: our dreams. When we are awake, our conscious mind is in charge. Most subtle insights or ideas coming from our unconscious are blocked by a barrier-like mechanism; they are not allowed to reach our consciousness. Hence, the unconscious is said to be *sub*merged. The reason we are equipped with such a mechanism is for the conscious mind to stay clear and focused. If this barrier was to be removed, we would become insane due to the amount of continuous information that would be unleashed, e.g., repressed feelings, emotions, memories, and all the colors we ever laid eyes upon. On the flip side, since the conscious mind is in charge, it can program the unconscious with input and, if the input is successful, the unconscious will steer all actions taken from our consciousness in the direction of the goal to reach – which would be the output. The unconscious will, indeed, constantly motivate us to reach the goal it has been programmed with. It is important to remember, however, that unlike our conscious mind, the unconscious makes no moral judgment. Therefore, it can be programmed with any kind of goal; be it good, evil, or even bad habits. Dreams are also the product of our unconscious. Since it never sleeps, when our conscious mind is on standby (sleeping), we are able to experience the countless images and symbols lying deep within our psyche; we enter the world of dreams.

Anthropologist Kilton Steward, in 1935, discovered a tribe living in the mountains of Malaysia. They were called *the Senoi*. This tribe had no history of mental illness, nor crime, although they lived amongst extremely violent headhunters. The Senoi were feared because they were thought to practice a powerful magic that affected the physical world. However, it was simply... *skillful dreams*. Instead of ignoring their dreams, like most cultures do, the Senoi always emphasized the understanding and discovery of this fantastic world. They even taught their children that dreams are a reality which must be understood and navigated. Take a look at the principles taught to every Senoi child:

- *Never run away from danger in a dream. Confront it and conquer it if necessary. If you are wounded, you have made your enemy use up part of its power. If you are killed, become reborn stronger.*
- *Call upon dream friends if you need help. Fight by yourself until they arrive. Make dream friends! Ask friendly figures to be your guides, share things in your dreams, e.g., food.*
- *A friend that acts aggressively toward you in a dream is not a friend, it is an enemy wearing the mask of a friend.*

- *After you have subdued or fought a dream opponent, make it give you a gift... something beautiful (a song or poem), or something useful. Bargain only if necessary.*
- *Advance toward pleasure in dreams.*
- *Achieve positive outcomes, help someone, fly someplace, do battle; act rather than react.*
- *If you act aggressively toward a friend or refuse to cooperate, go out of your way to express friendship or cooperation during waking.*

"You must relax and enjoy yourself when you fall in a dream. Falling is the quickest way to get in contact with the powers of the spirit world, the powers laid open to you through your dreams. Soon, when you have a falling dream, you will remember what I am saying, and as you do, you will feel that you are traveling to the source of the power which has caused you to fall."

"The falling spirits love you. They are attracting you to their land, and you have but to relax and to remain asleep in order to come to grips with them. When you meet them, you may be frightened of their terrific power, but go on. When you think you are dying in a dream, you are only receiving the powers of the other world; your own spiritual power which has been turned against you and which now wishes to become one with you, if you will accept it."

Dream Theory in Malaya
Kilton Steward, in Altered States of Consciousness

Why did the headhunters think that the Senoi performed powerful magic that affected their physical world? Well, because their spirit and intuitive mind were so closely attuned that it offered them not only surprisingly strong intuition, but also the faculty of perceiving things by means other than the known senses. This is the essence of the core of our being, and a precious gift that we seem to have forgotten, in favor of societies bent heavily on rationality. The reason I am emphasizing how the dream world affects our daily lives is because dreams are a reflection of our mind. If our five senses are the messengers of the brain, then intuition is the emissary of the soul; the portrayal of which is seen in, amongst other things, our dreams. In them, we even see a beautiful representation of creativity. Take, for example, the Scottish novelist *Robert Loui Stevenson*, the author of *Treasure Island*, and *Dr. Jekyll and Mr. Hyde,* who was inspired by his dreams. The same is true for *Edgar Allen Poe*, author of many short stories and poems such as *The Raven*, and *The Telltale Heart*, who said that his dreams inspired many of his writings. Furthermore, the composer *Giuseppe Tartini* wrote his famous masterpiece *the Devil's Sonata* after dreaming of the Devil playing the violin at the foot of his bed. He explains it as follows: *"One night, in the year 1713 I dreamed I had made a pact with the devil for my soul. Everything went as I wished: my new servant anticipated my every desire. Among other things, I gave him my violin to see if he could play. How great was my astonishment on hearing a sonata so wonderful and so beautiful, played with such great art and intelligence, as I had never even conceived in my boldest flights of fantasy. I felt enraptured, transported, enchanted: my breath failed me, and I awoke. I immediately grasped my violin in order to retain, in part at least, the impression of my dream. In vain! The music which I at this time composed is indeed the best that I ever wrote, and I still call it the 'Devil's Trill', but the difference between it and that which so moved me is so great that I would have destroyed my instrument and have said farewell to music forever if it had been possible for me to live without the enjoyment it affords me."*

Moreover, French philosopher and writer *Voltaire* composed his epic poem *La Henriade* in a dream. The same is true for the famous poems of *Samuel Taylor Coleridge*, *Kubla Khan*, and *The Rhyme of the Ancient Mariner*; they were inspired by dreams. We even see this phenomenon in the world of science. For example, the molecular structure of benzene was envisioned by German chemist *Friedrich A. Kekulé* in a dream. Also, Nineteenth century chemist *Dimitri Mendeleyev* once fell asleep while listening to music. In a dream, he saw that the basic chemical elements are all related in a fashion similar to the relation of notes in music. Based on that vision, Mendeleyev put together the entire periodic table in use today. The famous *Niels Bohr* is no exception, as he understood how electrons remain in their orbit around the nucleus of an atom, based on a vivid dream about horses running around a race track. Winning a Nobel Prize, he proposed one of quantum theories most prominent breakthroughs. Swiss psychiatrist *Carl Jung* also once said: *"All my works, all my creative activity, has come from those initial fantasies and dreams which began in 1912, almost fifty years ago. Everything that I accomplished in later life was already contained in them, although at first only in the form of emotions and images"*. Last but not least, Albert Einstein's special theory of relativity has a very similar story. In a dream, Einstein saw himself sledding down a steep mountainside, at a speed approaching that of light, when the appearance of the stars in the sky suddenly changed. This dream could very well have been the initial mental picture that ended up revolutionizing the way we think of space, time, and light. We have been gifted the ability to investigate and methodically observe the unseen. All this using an entity which is itself invisible. The potential of our mind is simply amazing.

This led me to a very interesting realization: if, as mentioned earlier, worship and prayer also initiate synaptic circuitry in the brain, which ultimately turns into thoughts and inclinations, then it must also be the vehicle that leads us to the source of our existence. I thought to myself, *if the strength of the circuitry increases with worship, this intensity must translate into something tangibly meaningful. The connection with the creator and sustainer of our universe must also increase as a result, until a singularity is achieved, i.e., in purpose, I become one with the creator.* We saw earlier that *we are our synapses*, but they seem to also be the medium through which God becomes manifest in every input we receive. This affects our reactions and, in turn, our destiny. And then it struck me! In Islam, there are messages from God directly to mankind known as *sacred discussions*. I instantly remembered one of them:

> *"My servant, obey me and you will be like me.*
> *You will tell something to be... and it will be."*

As such, Islam wants every individual to not only constantly remember that they are on trial for every input and output, but also that our potential – *through obedience* – is unlimited. It is this jurisprudence that I found fascinating. It causes every human, in possession of any type of sensory input, to carry an individual responsibility to righteousness against wickedness, and to keep in the forefront of our mind our preeminent potential. This is true not only concerning our own singular life, but also pertaining to the communal life in this world, i.e., human or otherwise. Perhaps the second best way to understand this reality is by remembering the patience and virtues of *Prophet Ayoub* (Job), and how God protected his cerebral prowess. I say *second best* because there is actually a much more profound example advocated later in the book.

Ayoub was wealthy, and lived a happy life with his wife and children. However, because he was very close and devoted to God, he became the target of the devil. Satan told God that Ayoub was thankful only because of the blessings bestowed upon him in this world. He continued saying that if these blessings were to be revoked, Ayoub would reveal his true character and no longer be thankful. Therefore, he requested from God to allow him to attack Ayoub, depriving him from his wealth and children, in order to prove that he would not remain pious thereafter. God gave him permission and Satan descended to do what he could to deprive the prophet from his wealth and children. To Satan's surprise, Ayoub remained steadfast in piety and thanksgiving; his synapses firmly rooted, attuned with the core of his being. Satan then requested permission to attack his body. God, again, gave him permission, except his senses and his mind, forbidding him from controlling these aspects of human beings. And although Satan was once more successful, rendering Prophet Ayoub very ill for a long time, the prophet still remained steadfast in piety and thanksgiving. As we can see, our mental aptitude is our weapon against the evil of any devil. It is through sensory input that our mind decides what is right from wrong, and God judges based on this decision. Therefore,

Satan's access to this aspect of human lives is prevented. Hence, the mind is our greatest gift, corrupted only if we allow it to be.

Have you ever noticed how, sometimes, if someone is staring at the back of our head, we suddenly turn around to see? What is that? Pure coincidence? Extra sensory perception? Well, I propose that this is a glimpse upon something that we possess as human beings seldom studied or researched, i.e., a capacity to *see*, tremendously more powerful than any of our physical senses. Indeed, we have been given the ability to interpret and formulate using something far greater than the mere messengers that are our five senses. Our mind can categorically not only personify the epitome of moral judgment, but also develop the immense potential of its transcendental perception, known in Arabic as *Baseerah*. This limitless perception allows us to clearly see beyond the obvious. Even more, to see clearly when our eyes are shut. This potential has been gifted to us, and we have further been enticed to exploit it. It ill befits us to ignore such a marvelous power anyway. Hence, we are responsible, culpable, and answerable, in the evident light of our capacity to choose what we do with such potential. If, as we have seen, that which our senses perceive is not absolute, then reality must be visualized through the individual sanctum that lies within each and every one of us. The journey is inward; toward the core of our being.

What lies within?

"Your sickness is from you, but you do not perceive it, and your remedy is within you, but you do not sense it. You presume that you are a small entity, but the entire universe is unfolded within you. You are, indeed, the evident book by whose alphabet the hidden becomes manifest. Thus, you have no need to look beyond yourself. What you seek is within you... If only you reflect."

– Imam Ali, son of Abi Taleb

* ~ * ~ * ~ * ~ * ~ * ~ * ~ * ~ *

Chapter 2

CORRUPTED LINKS

T he mind is the interpreter of any information we receive. That much is now understood to carry its own set of connotations. But how does it process this information? Well, it does so based on references to its extensive database, i.e., the memory of past experiences. For this reason, if the number three is brought up in a conversation, for example, it will not make sense unless it relates to a particular concept. Three what? Three pounds, meters, or people? The same is true for size. Is an ant big or small? Well, compared to an atom? An ant is huge! In fact, our entire existence is governed by this type of relativity. We understand things by comparison. We know *"good"* because of evil. We know health because of illness. We acknowledge and understand things because of what they are not. For instance, I know that the keyboard on which I am typing this page is a keyboard because it is not something else. And I know that the desk on which it sits is a desk because, amongst other things, it is not a keyboard. And I know that the place I am currently in is my office because it is not my living room. Such is our cognitive process, further affected by the lens through which we experience our reality. But what *is* reality? As seen in the previous chapter, our senses are not the temple of veracity, but only the faculty through which impressions are conveyed. Hence, reality is something I like to call: *confirmed information*. Although the following question will seem strange, please entertain the unfamiliar concept for a few moments before reading further, for the sake of understanding a very enlightening truth:

Who chooses your feelings and emotions?

Let us think about this question some more. Is it not possible that what made you cry yesterday, although now in the unaltered past, might make you feel normal today? And perhaps the memory of that same event might make you laugh tomorrow? Who chooses which of these feelings is engaged? *You* do. Indeed, the undertones of our perceptions are subjective. Because we understand things by comparison, and our internal lens affects the outcome, reality is ultimately what we make of it; reality is ultimately… *a choice.*

$$* \sim * \sim * \sim * \sim * \sim * \sim * \sim * \sim *$$

Trent and Dolores – The Sheikh and the Doctor
Tales of Broken Hearts, and the Power of Emotions

During his service in the Korean War, Trent Winstead wrote to Dolores, *"I'm awful glad to hear from you"*. Although they had just met a few weeks before he left for duty, they grew very fond of each other. Trent proposed to Dolores while she was brushing her teeth to make it harder for her to say no. They lived to see the birth of two children, three grandchildren, and no less than eight great grandchildren. Fondness grew and grew. They were deeply in love with one another. Even after retirement, they were always together, much more in love then when they were younger. The Washington Post newspaper interviewed their daughter Sheryl, *"It sounds so simple but it was so sweet,"* she remembered. *"They loved each other through the humdrum days. They were more and more in love every day,"* she said. The end of their story, however, is heart breaking. And I mean that literally. When Trent barely ate for several days because he constantly felt nauseated, his daughter, despite his reluctance to visit the doctor, urged him to go to the hospital and have himself checked. After the diagnosis, he was admitted to intensive care for Kidney failure. He needed dialysis. As time passed, Dolores found out that Trent's condition was declining. His heart was getting weaker because of the treatment he underwent. Trent was dying and Dolores knew it. The very next day in her husband's hospital room, she seemingly fell asleep. And although fairly healthy for her age, little did the Winstead family know, she was suffering from a severe case of brain hemorrhaging. The hospital allowed for their beds to be put in the same room next to each other. They held hands. Trent was initially admitted December 6th. Only three days later, at 9:10 pm on December 9th, about five weeks before their 64th anniversary, Eddie Winstead sentimentally told his dying father, *"She's passed on, Dad"*. Trent could not handle the loss of his beloved wife. *"We just watched him die,"* Sheryl painfully said. But what happened to Dolores? She was in good health, with no prior headaches or any signs of concern. Trent might have died of the complications caused by his kidney failure, and the treatment he received surely caused more harm, but Dolores' death, on the other hand, was completely due to a *broken heart*.

The Washington Post explains: "In 1990, Japanese physician *Hikaru Sato* wrote a thought-provoking paper describing an unusual set of sudden, life-threatening symptoms he and his colleagues were seeing in their patients. They included chest pain, shortness of breath, an elevated electrocardiogram and elevated cardiac enzyme levels. It looked very much like a heart attack. But when they delved deeper into what was going on, the doctors found that they were not signs of a heart attack and that their patients' arteries were clear. The condition was almost exclusive to women, and the women, as it happened, had recently undergone tremendous stress due to the loss of a loved one or other emotional event. In delving further into the mystery, they theorized that the left ventricle of the heart, which has the main responsibility for pumping, was weakened and mimicking the symptoms of a heart attack. Sato dubbed the condition *Takotsubo cardiomyopathy*, a name derived from an octopus trap because of the left ventricle's shape, which has been described as similar to a kind of fishing pot in Japan that has a round bottom, with a narrow neck that makes it difficult for a catch to escape. But since then, the illness has become more popularly known by a different name: *broken-heart syndrome*. Researchers now accept that this condition is a real one and not just one of soap operas and myths. A study in the *New England Journal of Medicine*, published in 2005, is among those that confirmed that a flood of stress hormones may be able to 'stun' the heart to produce heart spasms in otherwise healthy people. Another in 2011 in the journal *Coronary Artery Disease* described how the condition appears to be more common in post-menopausal women, and suggested that their lack of estrogen may make them more vulnerable. In most patients, the symptoms go away after a few weeks, and they recover fully. Others can face more serious complications, such as heart failure. Death is rare, but possible. Over the years, doctors have documented numerous cases of pairs of husbands and wives and parents and children dying shortly after one another. Takotsubo cardiomyopathy may be partly to blame. Earlier this month, Trent and Dolores Winstead, a Nashville couple married for 63 years, died hours apart in the same hospital room. This week, Carrie Fisher's mother, Debbie Reynolds, died the day after her daughter. Although little information has been released about the cause, numerous fans and friends of both actresses have gone online to comment that Reynolds may have died of a broken heart. George Takei, best known for his role as Mr. Sulu on the series *Star Trek*, tweeted: *There is nothing harder than having to bury a child. Debbie died of a broken heart, but she's with her daughter now."*

If our feelings and emotions could be strong enough to create a physiological phenomenon that mimics a heart attack, a stroke, or even brain hemorrhaging, then it is safe to conclude that they are also strong enough to not only affect our understanding of things, but also our reactions to them. This reality is also clearly seen in the *placebo effect*, in which a fake treatment using an inactive substance like water has been shown to improve patients' conditions, as long as they have a strong conviction that the treatment will cure them. As such, the outcomes of our experiences, as well as our understanding of things, are based much more on our pre-existing tendencies and the way we react, than on ***only*** what happens to us in its raw form. As Charles R. Swindoll puts it, *"The longer I love, the more I realize the impact of attitude on life. Attitude, to me, is more* *important than facts. It is more important than the past, than education, than money, than circumstances, than failures, than successes, than what other people think or say or do. It is more important than appearance, giftedness or skill. It will make or break a company... a church... a home. The remarkable thing is we have a choice every day regarding the attitude we will embrace for that day. We cannot change our past... we cannot change the fact that people will act in a certain way. We cannot change the inevitable. The only thing we can do is play on the one string we have, and that is our attitude... I am convinced that life is 10% what happens to me and 90% how I react to it. And so it is with you... we are in charge of our attitudes."*

A Muslim scholar (*sheikh*) was once preaching to a group of doctors about the impact that the words of the Qur'an have on the human body. He explained that if someone has a headache, for example, reading a few verses of the Qur'an could sooth and dissipate the ailment. A person in the audience, with the pre-existing tendencies of a doctor that believes in facts and tangible treatments, relayed his objection aloud, abruptly interrupting the speaker, *"That's nonsense!"* he said. *"We too believe in the power of the word of God, but taking the matter to this extreme is not only wishful, but also dangerous! What if that person was having a sudden case of brain hemorrhaging? What then would words be good for? With all due respect, no matter your religious background, sheikh, you do not really believe that mere words and sentences can have a tangibly measurable physical impact on the human body? Do you?"* To everyone's shock, the sheikh grinned and only said, *"You... are garbage."* The doctor became really angry, throwing a couple of insults as he grabbed his jacket before precipitously leaving the hall. As the angry doctor left, everybody else gathered toward the sheikh to inquire about his reaction to the situation, given the fact that he is known to have always had a much different, gentler, and calmer demeanor. After a long convoluted discussion, their unanimous decision was to have a group of them immediately visit the doctor's house, bringing the sheikh along, in order to resolve the issue between them. The sheikh agreed.

At the house, they all sat in the living room, quietly awaiting the sheikh's apology for having disrespected a highly regarded doctor in the community. Surprisingly, the doctor was calm and smiling. Probably because he felt he would reclaim his honor, knowing that the sheikh would apologize to him. After a few minutes, the sheikh finally looked at him and said, *"You... are garbage."* At that point, the doctor was furious. He stood, angrily yelling at the sheikh to leave his house. The sheikh stood and, to the doctor's surprise, said, *"I now apologize to you with all my heart, doctor. Please accept my humble apology, and I'll explain to you why I said this again. I actually have a very good reason."* The doctor swiftly relaxed, ostensibly realizing what the sheikh was about to say.

"I accept your apology..." he said reluctantly. The sheikh pointed out to him how the same mere words made him very angry twice, and the other apologetic sentence just now instantly calmed him down. The doctor was baffled, and his understanding of the entire situation suddenly dawned on him like a revelation.

On two occasions, the doctor's face changed from calm looking to furious, and from his usual skin color to a deep red. His heart must have been racing. His arterial tensions and testosterone levels must have increased tremendously, and his left brain hemisphere was no doubt bustling with stimuli. His physiology changed based on only three words: *"you... are garbage."* And these words were not even of divine origin. Yet there he was, a few hours prior in the hall, a doctor informed in biology, objecting to the fact that the words of almighty God could have a tangible beneficial impact on the body.

$$* \sim * \sim * \sim * \sim * \sim * \sim * \sim * \sim *$$

If human reality is ultimately a choice, and our attitude is *the one string we have to play on,* then we should recognize our vulnerability. Our cognitive system can be exploited and, if primed correctly, it is possible for us to be forced to perceive only that which our mind is inclined to understand. Do you see where I am going with this? As a deduction, although nature and nurture both contribute into making us who we are, not only does nurture play the bigger role, it also considerably shapes our thinking methodology. That is not to say that we see, smell, feel, hear, and taste differently from one another, but that our experiences end up being personalized based on our built in inclinations. But there is an even more obscure danger... I will try a little experiment with you in order to clarify where I am taking this notion. What if I had you make a choice, and then told you what you chose? As simple as that and with no strings attached. After all, how could there be? You are reading this book long after I wrote it, are you not?

Choose a number between 0 and 5.

When you have that number, flip the page...

Why 3?

I first have to admit that this does not always work. But if your number is indeed 3, then who made that choice? You or me? Well, in a way, we both did. You see, our brain likes to situate itself. Hence, when presented with a range, we usually choose the middle. My knowledge of this helped me prepare an experiment with a high probability of knowing what your choice would be, before you were even presented with the problem. I exploited this *vulnerability*. Can you imagine what could be done with this type of conditioning? This is something that we will delve deeper into in chapter 3, but I wanted to present it to you here in order to elaborate on something that fell victim to this treachery: Islam.

It is bacusee of this type of mental conditioning taht mnay poplee aunord the wrold tadoy see and urstadennd the rligeion of Ialsm diffreent than the way it aulatcly is. They see distortion where there is actually none. The course of Islam has been changed, erroneous information eventually became integral, and everything went awry. Who is the culprit for this distortion? I am glad you asked! Some individuals, organizations, corporations, as well as several media outlets – all versed in the human cognitive process – have mentally conditioned people in order to fulfill their economic and/or political agendas, following in the footsteps of the pharaohs in human history. Others are trying to convince people of their own false understanding of things based on certain biases. I was once watching the evening news when I saw two Muslim men in an interview with the channel, speaking about the effect of terrorism on society. They were condemning the perpetrators for being *"extremists"*. I frowned because there is no such thing as *extremism* in Islam. In fact, the religion actually warns against any form of radicalization, and the religious conduct that every Muslim should adopt is clearly explained without any form of ambiguity. Terrorists are not Muslims, nor do their acts have anything in common with Islam. I nonetheless continued watching, although I often change the channel or stop listening because it bothers me to see such nonsense constantly being televised. Had I only known what one of them was going to say next, I would have turned off the television altogether. Adding insult to injury, one of them said, *"...but we, moderate Muslims, are not like that!"* Moderate Muslims?! I could not believe my ears! Here is a *so called Muslim* on television, in front of millions of viewers, basically telling the world that the religion of Islam is evil. He, however, is *moderate* about it?! I would have loved this person to explain what part of Islam he is *"moderate"* about, given the fact that all the instances that mention war or violence in the Qur'an were specifically introduced to attend to very specific situations. You see, before the revelation of the Holy Qur'an, the world was filled with violence and oppression, and especially so in the Arabian Peninsula. Therefore, God provided solutions to Prophet Mohamad and the Muslims, some of which involved war against the oppressors, as well as preemptive measures for protection against them. These passages in the book are constantly taken out of this context, creating fear and hatred. The man on my TV screen was simply adding to the stigma. But as we shall soon see in this book, these wars were all in self-defense, protecting the weak and oppressed. Prophet Mohamad was commanded by God to fight very evil people, with whom all other peaceful means actually resulted in failure. Something that the prophet could not afford, for the sake of humanity... for the sake of the truth.

Indeed, many people's thoughts and inclinations have been *modeled* and, in turn, these people have influenced others to think alike, creating a snowball effect. The truth is bent. And although global awareness of this propaganda promulgation seems to be on the rise, there is also a catch. The *aware* usually thinks that, in the twenty first century, the truth has either been replaced by falsehood or has been altogether suppressed. However, the truth has actually been *disguised*, and this is a very important concept to understand. Upon further scrutiny, any intelligent person will realize that falsehood is actually in camouflage, *cloaked* as the truth. This is extremely dangerous, making people believe that falsehood needs to be upheld, all the while... they are being fooled into thinking that it is actually *the truth* that they are upholding.

Imagine the repercussions of such dilettantism. At best? Complacent arrogance. At worst? Complacent oppression! For obvious satanic reasons, the biggest victims of such oppression are the prophets of God, and the most affected of them is the final prophet, Mohamad. Unfortunately, even so called Muslim publications, often actually seeking to destroy his image, have been authored with lies ascribed to him, and many Muslims believe them. Suffice it to say that this deception occurs because of the reasons outlined. Paulo Coelho, the author of the book *The Winner Stands*

Alone, mentioned in his book a beautiful concept that can serve as an analogy here. He wrote:

> "Several biological studies have shown that a frog placed in a container along with water from its pond, will remain alive while you slowly heat the water. The toad does not react to the gradual increase of temperature (change of environment) and only dies when the water boils, swollen and happy. On the other hand, if a toad is thrown into that same container when the water is already boiling, it will immediately jump out. It will be a little singed, but alive! Sometimes we can be like the boiled toads. We do not notice changes. We think everything is good, or that whatever is evil will pass, it's just a matter of time. We are about to die, but we are floating, stable and apathetic as the water warms up every minute. We are dying, fat and happy, without having noticed the changes around us. There are boiled toads who still believe that the key is obedience, not competence: might is right, and obey whoever is sensible. From all this, where is the real life? It is better to emerge from a situation, maybe a little singed from time to time, but alive and ready to act."

As human beings, we owe it to ourselves to not be fooled by what we see and hear, and even worse, to not become apathetic to the fraud and exploitation happening around us. One should think, look into, cross reference, and confirm by understanding all the angles and intricacies of any belief system before forming an opinion on the subject. And this should be especially so if that subject impacts other people in our worldwide, diversified community. And this confirmation should not be from hearsay either. Many a times, certain people change the course of information pertaining to a subject, tainting it with fallacies, and such is the case with the religion of Islam. Furthermore, what adds insult to injury is the fact that Muslims have become satisfied with letting others represent their religion. Hence, these fallacies end up becoming part of the system because people – even those that have adopted the system – followed suit without any confirmation. Moreover, when new people are doing their research, they find these fallacies as part of the system, forming opinions based on distorted truth; they reject the idea, sadly, based on falsehood. The fact is that, in our day and age, a lot of this distortion exists not only with Islam, but actually in many other facets of our daily lives. This is the ultimate cause for all the world's confusion, misunderstanding, misinterpretation, misrepresentation, turmoil, smearing, exaggeration, misuse, and last but not least, stereotyping. The chain's corrupted links must be removed; restoring the truth.

"There will come a time when nothing will be hidden except the truth, and nothing will be revealed except falsehood."

– Imam Ali, son of Abi Taleb

~~*~*~*~*~*~*~*

Chapter 3

THE TWILIGHT OF FALSEHOOD

Name the word spelled by the following letters:

S - H - O - P

Quick: say the word aloud!

When driving, what do you do when you come to a green light?

Quick: say it aloud!

Stop? Are you sure? At a green light?

If you did indeed say (or think) *stop*, and a lot of people do, my mental conditioning succeeded. Here, similar to what I did with the number 3 of our previous experiment from chapter 2, I primed you to think of the opposite word. This is the power of suggestion manipulating our cerebral prowess. If you want to see this power at work for yourself, try it with other people. Ask them: w*hat is the word spelled S , H , O , P?* Then ask them: w*hat do you do when come to a green light?* You would be surprised at how many people are actually susceptible to this phenomenon. Mental conditioning manipulates people not only to act, but to also adhere to a particular thinking process. Let me show you this reality once more. How knowledgeable are you in world religions? I speculate that even if you have not attended a church, temple, synagogue, or a mosque in a long time, you should still be able to answer this fairly easy religious question: How many of each kind of animal did Moses bring on his ark? Pause for a second here, and answer the question...

You see, by eliciting your brain with words such as "world religions", "church", "temple", "synagogue", "mosque", "animal", and "ark", it becomes primed to directly access the necessary *religious information* needed to answer the question, often ignoring trivial details. However, in certain cases such as this one, the detail is far from trivial. In fact, Moses is not the right person! It is Noah. The same thing happens when I tell you that Mary's mother has four children: April, May, June and...? No. Not July. Her fourth child is Mary. Because the brain is dynamic, it constantly looks for arrangements, methods, and sequences that have continuations. Hence, it skips the *"Mary's mother"* section of the sentence in order to save energy for other more vital processes. This process could also be seen in the visual department:

Look at the above frame. Does anything about it strike you as odd, or altogether wrong? If not, look again. Nothing? Look once more.

The word *"you"* is repeated. Your brain might have ignored it because it is an unimportant detail for the understanding of the sentence. Simply put, the brain trades accuracy for efficiency. I sure hope that at least one of these experiments worked out in my favor. Otherwise, I can imagine you feeling all invincible right now. But that would still be ok because I am sure you caught my drift, and that alone is the first step toward protection against the real world situations which are not so cut and dry. A single frame in a movie playing at 48 frames per second will pass right under your conscious radar, but nonetheless be absorbed by your unconscious. That, for example, is the real danger. But why am I telling you all this? Good question! Well, for this very reason... this drawback could be exploited. This understanding of how the brain works, from the first chapter of this book when we delved into the microscopic level of neurons and synapses, until now when we looked at the overall macro consequences, should give you a sense of how dangerous priming the brain and eliciting thoughts with input that lies just under the threshold of human consciousness could be. The music industry today, for example, is filled with this kind of programming. Corporations also use this strategy to condition us to make a purchase, by simply repeating a catchy phrase a few times until it becomes imbedded in our unconscious. Also notice that at a hip-hop concert, if they did not know better, people might think that they are witnessing some sort of trans-inducing ritual, in which the audience is hypnotically repeating the words of the performer, occasionally even followed by weird gestures. Surely, if our mind was a tangible entity, it would resemble clay, ready to be sculpted by a potter. *And the astute will read between the lines...*

We sometimes believe things not out of conviction, but because we have been conditioned to believe them. Such are, in the case of children, for example, Santa Claus, the eastern bunny, and the tooth fairy. As for adults, how we look at a particular situation or piece of information is ultimately how we will see it. And this, to the victim, is a prison with invisible walls. The psychological elaborateness of mind-manipulation transposes the victim to a state in which the feeling of acting on one's own initiative is ever present. In our little exercise earlier, a person that gives the answer *"stop"* to the question *"what do you do when you come to a green light?"* is confident that they are speaking the truth. Hypothetically speaking, if people did not know and the idea of stopping at a green light spread, what would the repercussions be? Well, the system would change. Although the truth is that a person should *go* on a green light, the opposite would happen, and a foreign person visiting the country would be baffled by the way the traffic works, unaware of the *initial* truth or where this antagonistic civil engineering originated from. Although the truth needs no advocate, when a lie is told often enough it becomes the new truth; allusions, innuendos, and false interpretations – all with unrestricted access to the truth's wardrobe.

* ~ * ~ * ~ * ~ * ~ * ~ * ~ * ~ *

Light Upon Light

Enough light is needed to see, and without it nothing is revealed. That much is certain. And when we walk into a dark room, we search blindly for the light switch. However, once turned on, a blazing light blinds he who has weak eyes. *The truth* is a blazing light, and a lot of people have failed to exercise their esoteric vision. Many a time, the intensity of the truth is blinding because we have become complacent to the gentle glow of falsehood, which seemingly renders everything beautiful. To cope with the blazing light, we must evoke our *Baseerah*, which would allow us to finally see what it reveals; *we have to close our eyes.* In fact, a vivid eyesight is flawed if our insight is dead! In other words, we have to care for the truth, seeking it with all our emotional might. Yes, as we will soon see when more pages of this book have turned, our emotions are a function to be reckoned with. With eyes complacently wide open, we are blind to the truth in favor of what is seemingly easy to see. And although the misleading twilight of falsehood – ostensibly beautiful – has many advocates, the afterglow of deception will never extinguish the luminous light of truth:

"They wish to extinguish the light of Allah with their mouths, but Allah refuses, and instead perfects His light, despite the hatred of the disbelievers. It is He who sent His messenger

in guidance, and with the religion of truth, to manifest it over all of the religion, despite the hatred of the idolaters."

– Qur'an 9:32, 33

In Islam, the branches of falsehood have germinated independently from the initial seed of truth. Therefore, if the false branches are removed, the truth will easily be revealed. The problem is that, for some, falsehood has become more cogent than the truth itself.

As for Muslims, we have been instructed by God to continually read, research, confirm, think, and finally compare and contrast. Everything should make sense. Everything should be *confirmed information*. And if reality is information, everything should be *real*. Hence, the very first verses revealed to Prophet Mohamad in the Qur'an are as follows:

"Read in the name of thy Lord who created. Created man from a clot. Read, and thy Lord is most generous. He who taught with the pen. Taught man what he knew not."

– Qur'an 96:1 – 5

However, many Muslims have forgotten that even if a person is born of Muslim parents, they have been commanded by God to continually read, learn, and confirm, in order to own a belief of conviction, which alone shall be accepted by God. Thus, no one can claim to be a Muslim merely by heredity, or because of being born in a Muslim family and/or community. Furthermore, any religious information, ruling, or code of conduct and demeanor, should come directly from God, or from those that are deeply rooted in knowledge. Unfortunately, many Muslims today take their religion lightly, based on their own personal preferences and opinions, as well as false traditions and erroneous information that had been forcefully contrived into it.

Before the advent of Prophet Mohamad, during his life, after his death, and to this day, Satan's minions have worked very hard to taint the truth with false ideologies, false traditions, and false allegiances. The irony is that although non-Muslims view the religion of Islam based on the actions of Muslims, many *so called Muslims* today have deviated from the true path of the religion, which also contributes to the disfigurement. Sadly, these people are heedless of the harm they are causing. Indeed, many *Muslims* are no longer Muslims, and the worst part is that they do not even know.

But if the truth has been muffled and falsehood is roaming free, how then does one know? How are the chain's false links discovered, and how to ultimately remove them? The answer is: by comparing any aspect of the system with a frame of reference, in order to correlate any information received pertaining to it. This frame should not be simply allusions and innuendos, but an unprecedented decree specifically designed by God as a guideline of instructions to establish, guide, rectify, instruct, and certify. While seeking the truth, we initially need to carry with us *something* that will overcome the twilight of falsehood and illuminate our way. Reverting to common sense, this *something* evidently becomes a group of personalities established as exemplars by our creator; role models. And to *carry personalities*, we have to exercise our emotional intelligence, and evoke their essence in our soul. Our synapses will be affected as a result. But **who are** these personalities? In order to answer this question, we have to look at a very interesting verse in the Qur'an in which light is specifically mentioned as *"light upon light"*. This verse is known as *the verse of light*, and its understanding will exercise our emotional intelligence, and open our soul to house the essence of the personalities it refers to. Doing so will awake our transcendental perception, and make us ready to receive increasingly incandescent light to illuminate our life:

> *"Allah is the light of the heavens and the earth, His light resembles a niche within which is a cresset. The cresset is within glass. The glass is as though it were a brilliant globe, lit from a blessed olive tree neither eastern nor western, the oil of which is seemingly illuminated even if no fire has*

touched it. Light upon light, Allah offers guidance to whom He wills. And Allah gives examples to people. And Allah is knowing of all things." – **Qur'an 24:35**

I promised to introduce you to the ambassadors of truth, and the interpretation of the verse of light could very well be the best introduction. The verse says, "*...a niche within which is a cresset,"* and the *niche* is *Fatima Al-Zahraa*, Prophet Mohamad's daughter. It continues saying, *"...within which is a cresset,"* referring to her son *Imam Al-Hassan Al-Mojtaba*. Further it says, "*The cresset is within glass,"* referring to his younger brother *Imam Al-Hussein Al-Shaheed*. Furthermore, it continues with, *"lit from a blessed olive tree,"* which refers to them being from the blessed lineage of Prophet Abraham. Moreover, "[the tree] *neither eastern nor western,"* confirms that Abraham was not Jewish, nor was he Christian; he was Muslim, as were all the prophets starting with Adam, the first prophet of God. Finally, we see, *"Light upon light,"* showing that the genealogy of these personalities provided one leader after another; guidance upon guidance (Note: the Arabic word *Imam* means leader):

The prophet of God Mohamad, son of Abdullah

His daughter Fatima *Al-Zahraa*

Imam Ali, son of Abi Taleb – Fatima Al-Zahraa's husband

Their son *Imam* Al-Hassan *Al-Mujtaba*

His younger brother *Imam* Al-Hussein *Al-Shaheed*

The progeny of Al-Hussein:

Imam Ali *Zein-Alabedeen*, son of Al-Hussein

Imam Mohamad *Al-Baqer*, son of Ali

Imam Jafar *Al-Sadeq*, son of Mohamad

Imam Moussa *Al-Qadem*, son of Jafar

Imam Ali *Al-Reda*, son of Moussa

Imam Mohamad *Al-Jawad*, son of Ali

Imam Ali *Al-Hadi*, son of Mohamad

Imam Al-Hassan *Al-Askari*, son of Ali

Imam Mohamad *Al-Mahdi*, son of Al-Hassan

As seen here, they are a total of fourteen – light upon light – giving the fruit of their knowledge every now and again:

> *"Do you not see how Allah gave an example, the similitude of a good word is like that of a good tree whose root is firmly fixed with branches in the sky? It gives its fruit every now and again by permission of its Lord, and Allah gives examples to people so that they may be reminded."*
>
> **– Qur'an 14:24, 25**

God, who has created man from a simple drop of liquid form, which he powerfully turned into a clinging clot and artistically molded into male and female, is indeed all knowing. If Islam is the ultimate truth, then he **must** have protected it by establishing a frame of reference to refer to for confirmation of any information received.

He has...

"The truth is with us," he said confidently, *"...and in us,"* he continued. This confidence stems from his statute established by almighty God. He further continued, *"Whoever says this other than us is a liar and a forger."* This man is not only from the lineage of the holy Prophet Mohamad, but he also shares his name. Indeed, *Imam* Mohamad *Al-Mahdi*, currently in occultation, is the twelfth of these leaders, as seen in the genealogy above.

In this occultation, he is protected by God until an appointed day.

God promised his reappearance on that day…

And God fulfills his promises.

* ~ * ~ * ~ * ~ * ~ * ~ * ~ * ~ *

"Pray more for my reappearance.

Because in it... is your salvation."

– *Imam* Mohamad *Al-Mahdi*

~ PART TWO ~

ETERNAL INFINITY

The story of creation… and that of our purpose.

Now that part one is just abaft our consciousness, I hope to have –
maybe indirectly – successfully conveyed to you how foreign we are
in a world that has been fabricated.

In part two here, we delve into reasoning, and I promise that some
very deep philosophical questions you might have asked yourself
will be answered in some way. Together in this part, we will
understand existence. Forgive the simple math we will do, and trust
that it is necessary. I will take you back in time to before even the
beginning – I will prove the existence of God. This part of the book is
reminiscent to dusting off a painting, refurbishing it to its initial
allure. When this restoration process has been completed, I will invite
you to take a few steps back, in order to see more of God's masterpiece:
the Truth.

In this part, we quiet all conventional inhibitions, and delve into
human consciousness at its purest form.

"And this living world is only diversion and amusement. And it is the home of the Hereafter that is the real life... if only they knew."

– Qur'an 29:64

Chapter 4
BEFORE THE BEGINNING

Of a beginning, things are made. The existence of something entails its beginning. But what of *before* the beginning? Where did everything in existence come from? Was everything created by a pre-existing creator, or did everything start from nothing? It is imperative to begin by answering these questions because our origin matters in the search for the truth. You see, if we were not created, but simply came to exist from ecological change that started from nothing and evolved because of natural selection, we would have no prescribed purpose because we came from nothing and are going to end up as nothing after death as well. Consequently, the search for truth would specifically be influenced by this mentality because questions such as *"why are we here?"* and *"what is our purpose?"* become irrelevant. For example, why would atheists ponder upon why they exist? If they believe that they came from *nothing* and are going to *nothing*, then there is no reason for their existence in the first place. To them, it was simply a random sequence of events resulting in our existence; pure chance, with no reason for *it*, nor purpose for *them*. If, on the other hand, we were actually created, then questions such as *"who/what created us?"* and *"what is the purpose of this creation?"* as well as *"what is required of us?"* become not only important, but also essential. These things considered, how do we know which questions to ask? Thereupon lies the importance of the initial question: *where did everything in existence come from in the first place?* In other words, *does God exist?* Well, there has always been unequivocal proof for the existence of God! Nonetheless, I will present new proof for the existence of a creator and sustainer to our universe in an upcoming chapter. Prior to that, however, allow me in this current chapter to quash some of the arguments presented by atheists in their discussions and debates. This will act as a framework to the understanding of specific concepts, as well as for the sake of completion. Once these arguments have been addressed, I will prove the existence of God logically, mathematically, as well as scientifically. Henceforth, the question of whether or not God exists will no longer be a debate – if it ever was.

$$* \sim * \sim * \sim * \sim * \sim * \sim * \sim * \sim *$$

The Failure of Atheism

Some atheists argue, saying that Charles Darwin solved one of the greatest riddles, presenting the possibility of getting something from nothing. I take issue with this claim! Charles Darwin only **proposed** a **theory** explaining how organisms **could have** changed or *evolved* during the history of life on earth. Therefore, his work is known not as *the **law** of evolution*, but rather as *the **theory** of evolution*. Whereas, for contrasting example, the work of French chemist and microbiologist *Louis Pasteur* – renowned for his discoveries of the principles of vaccination, as well as microbial fermentation and pasteurization – is known as *the **law** of biogenesis*. This law demonstrates that complex living things come only from other living things. Thus, modern life does not arise from non-living material, let alone from nothing. Furthermore, even Charles Darwin himself alluded in his work that life must have been created! Take a look at the following excerpt from the famous last paragraph of his book *On the Origin of Species*:

> *"There is grandeur in this view of life, with its several powers, **having been originally breathed** into a few forms or into one; and that, whilst this planet has gone cycling on according to the fixed law of gravity, from so simple a*

beginning, endless forms most beautiful and most wonderful have been, and are being, evolved. " **– Charles Darwin**

Moreover, in subsequent editions of the book, Darwin edited this paragraph to include a stunning statement. Take a look:

> *"There is grandeur in this view of life, with its several powers, **having been originally breathed by the Creator** into a few forms or into one; and that, whilst this planet has gone cycling on according to the fixed law of gravity, from so simple a beginning, endless forms most beautiful and most wonderful have been, and are being, evolved. "*
>
> **– Charles Darwin**

Again, as is evidently indisputable, Charles Darwin did not offer a solution for the origin of life, as he himself even says that life was *"originally breathed by the creator"*. Rather, he proposed a theory about how organisms *might* have evolved into the many creatures that exist on the planet. In spite of this, however, many atheists (or more accurately *evolutionists)* still argue that every time a new specie is created, it is *"something from nothing"*, putting words in Darwin's mouth. I ask: what philosophy is this? What of space, time, and the planet? What about genetics... are *they* nothing? As a matter of fact, a person giving this argument would have to be living in a *vacuum environment* in order for it to hold any legitimacy. Furthermore, the astute will sometimes notice atheists make use of the word **created** in their sentences, just as Darwin did. Does not this word mean built, conceived, constructed, designed, devised, made, brought into being, brought into existence, brought to pass, caused to be, given birth to, given life to? Are they confused?

No, they are not...

You see, every human being has an instinctive belief in a designer and sustainer to our existence. God has imbued the apprehension of his presence in every one of us. In atheists, on the other hand, this instinctive belief is usually suppressed because they are dispassionate about the existence of a creator. More importantly, they are passionate about the idea of the non-existence of God, due to the fact that the lens through which they view the subject is tainted with false understanding, sometimes even making the proposition seem evil. They convince themselves that God does not exist, because they failed to find the truth, contending that the arguments presented by the believers in God are absurd, contain many contradictions, and have no tangible evidence. I do not blame them for their illusion of disbelief in the existence of God because they might not have been introduced to the ultimate truth – *yet*. In contrast, I certainly blame them for their bold conviction of opinion, based *only* on what they know. What about what they *do not* know? If an archeologist is looking for a particular tree in a forest, can he justifiably say that he has not found the tree, based on having searched *only* half of the forest? Of course not! It is, indeed, less than adequate to form the opinion of the nonexistence of God without first having become learned in at least most major religions of the world, as well as all their intricacies. Yet again, you find devout atheists arguing that God does not exist, while their knowledge about world religions is only from hearsay; incomplete and filled with falsehood. Whoever seeks to find the truth with a sound, unbiased, and impartial open mind – and a scoop of good intentions – will eventually find it. And this is because the truth itself is also seeking these minds.

For the reasons outlined, I do not believe atheists when they say that they do not believe in God. Rather, I know that deep down inside every atheist lies the recognition of a designer and sustainer to our multiverse, but they are angry with him. They dislike the idea of being servants to God. They refuse to accept the fact that they have been created and should worship their creator. However, because this instinct was instilled by God, and because it is deeply a part in every one of us, so called atheists always show a very typical behavior that the adroit observer will notice; they unconsciously divulge their natural belief in a creator, time and time again. Hence, we hear them say that species are *created*.

If Darwin's theory of evolution is true, why can we not see it happening right now? The answer that evolutionists give is that the process is too slow for us to see. They say that it has been twenty five million years since we have had an ape for an ancestor. Therefore, they contend that the average human lifetime is too short to see evolution in progress. I say: if it is too slow for us to see; if that presumption is true, where is the proof for its validity? If they cannot see it, then they are only speculating, are they not? Unfortunately for them, speculation does not equate to evidence.

Many try to counter this by saying, for example, that we can see evolution in bacteria. I was shocked to hear this argument. You see, they fail to understand that bacteria resistance to antibiotic is not *evolution*. It is *variation*. One of the causes for bacteria resistance to antibiotics is Horizontal Gene Transfer (HGT). HGT is the movement of genetic material between unicellular and/or multicellular organisms, other than through the transmission of DNA, from one of the former – or the latter – to another of them. This argument can actually be answered by asking a simple question: if evolution is seen in bacteria, what then does bacteria *"evolve"* into? It is still bacteria, is it not? Yes it is... I rest my case!

With these aspects brought to light, I am actually glad that my doctor does **not** have any *Darwinian wits* about him, and it is no disgrace for a doctor to say that he or she does not believe in evolution, simply because there is no evidence for it. Quite the contrary, because doctors would have to otherwise betray their common sense in order to believe that something evolves into itself!?

Furthermore, why is there a complete lack of transitional forms altogether? As in, why is it that there are only either Humans and Apes, but no Apemans and Humapes? Why are there no Kigers and Tats, but only – quite distinctly – Tigers and Cats? In fact, the entire process of the theory of evolution is completely vacant of such intermediaries! Not only are these links indeed missing from the observable world we live in today, but they are also unsurprisingly missing from any recorded fossil throughout history; nowhere to be found! Yet, despite these striking facts, atheists/evolutionists are working very hard to try and keep evolution in schools – pure betrayal of common sense.

The irony is that many famed atheists are actually scientists. It is ironic because if we look at scientific laws such as those of thermodynamics, for example, which is the arm of science that deals with the relationship between heat and other forms of energy, we see that these laws completely contradict the theory of evolution and unequivocally demonstrate its lack of validity. For instance, the second law of thermodynamics (a.k.a. entropy) states that a system comprised of atoms or molecules breakup and disorganize, as opposed to organize and evolve. This is one of many examples of straightforward proof that Darwin's theory of evolution is just that: a theory. In light of this, and since there is no tangible evidence that living organisms evolve – and also that there is, on the other hand, much undisputable proof against it – anyone with a little bit of common sense will confidently conclude that Charles Darwin's theory of evolution is false.

Nonetheless, in defiance of these firmly established facts, atheists still argue that nothing suggests *design*. They say that things look designed until you take a closer look at them and realize all the faults. For example, one such *"fault"* they often mention is that of the *Recurrent Laryngeal Nerve*. They criticize how it goes down into the chest and loops back up again, rather than going straight to its end organ. This argument is very poor for several reasons, and you do not have to be a surgeon to understand them. First of all, science is still trying to comprehend many biological functions of the human body. Therefore, until we have a clear understanding of all its intricacies, no one can rightfully criticize any of its features because, based on common sense, that person must first understand the system in its entirety. As far as the human system is concerned, no one does! Secondly, criticizing a particular feature of any system also suggests that a better design exists. This would be impossible for anyone to propose because no one fully understands how or why we grow our organs and body parts the way we do. Let me clarify… In order to present an improved Laryngeal Nerve design, one would logically have to come up with a replacement *"organogenic"* developmental design, starting from the fertilized ovum to the fetus and beyond, accounting for all the causes, sparks, molecular activity, as well as all the anatomical convolutions. How crazy would that be?

Which brings me to my next point: embryology. Embryonic development is one of the most fascinating transformations that will continue to baffle scientists throughout the foreseeable future. Indeed, the autonomy of our cells at this stage is an awe inspiring process, and our prenatal advancement of gamete into a complete human body is nothing short of extraordinary. The intricate scheme by which our system of body parts and organs form during the early stages of development is fascinating, because the arrangement of our system has to take into account countless factors affecting the process. One of these factors is what I like to call *the setup*. Imagine someone preparing a horse and carriage setup to travel somewhere, putting the carriage before the horse. He will not get very far, will he? Of course not! He will not even start moving because his setup is flawed and no further development can or will occur. And this is just with a very simple transportation system! Can you imagine this predicament with the intricacies of all the parts, organs, and functions of the entire human body? Any intelligent person will not fail to appreciate how precisely calculated the initial setup has to be, as well as how many precise calculations need to be considered in order to avoid any problems, interference, interruptions, impediments, and so on. Furthermore, every individual entity has to be free to not only grow unrestricted to its full potential, but also consider its relation to the other entities of the system.

As such, keeping in mind that we might discover an even greater amount of reasons in the future, our current knowledge shows that the laryngeal nerve's length, location, as well as routing, actually happen to be the way they are because of several intelligent design reasons. Some currently known reasons are to avoid developmental constraints, to adjust and calibrate laryngeal functions, as well as to offer extra protection against injury. Hence, perfect design.

Atheists are blind to these truths because they are kept in a cage of distorted awareness, taking *only* what seems obvious into consideration. They inadequately eliminate all possibilities for the existence of God, based only on a handful of experiences. They are the archeologists looking for a tree, arguing that it does not exist based on having searched only half of the forest. This is on the one hand. On the other, I congratulate them. And no, I am not being sarcastic, nor am I mocking them. I mean this congratulation wholeheartedly because by saying, *"there is no God,"* they have taken the first step toward the truth. Many, if not all atheists have embraced their ideologies because they eventually found flaws in the religion in which they were brought up – or the religion their parents followed for that matter. My commendation to them is due to the fact that instead of being blindly enthralled by the twilight of falsehood, they actively shaped their neurologic circuitry; they asked questions. Subsequently, instead of putting their brain on the side, they wanted God to make sense to them, and that is what I appreciate, i.e., a beneficial *active skepticism*. Instead of being gullible, beguiled by those who are versed in the human cognitive process – or worse, succeeding those who judge and decide solely based on their biases – these atheists have taken action. *"There is no god,"* they blithely said. The problem is that they stopped there, now forming their own prejudice. How ironic is that? Not to know is detrimental, but worse is not to wish to know! And many atheists have closed their ears, stuck in their half of the forest. On the other hand, a Muslim **also says**: *"There is no God..."* but follows through with, *"except Allah."*

* ~ * ~ * ~ * ~ * ~ * ~ * ~ * ~ *

Free Will

Is free will an illusion? Do we really have *a choice*? Many atheists mention this argument quite frequently. In fact, the issue of whether or not we have free will has been a debate for thousands of years. Their altercation is that, based on neurological studies, our mind appears to be making decisions before we are actually aware of them. Hence, we do not have free will, but only an illusion of it. They say, *"to choose your thoughts, you'd have to think them before you thought them"*. I find this somewhat interesting because, upon further investigation, one will undoubtedly realize that this belief is, at its core, contradictory of itself. Actually, it is begging the question, only saying that choices are not choices. It is like saying that the color blue is not blue, but it is only blue because we see it as blue. In order for any intelligent being to objectively propose such a nihilistic argument, one that has to do with his very being, he would have to first subjectively think about it, would he not? Imagine you are in a restaurant, and the menu offers fifteen different meals to choose from. So that you may objectively ascertain whether the choice you make would actually involve free will, you would have to be in complete harmony with your being and first and foremost **subjectively** choose. Otherwise, how would you be able to ponder upon whether or not it was free will? In other words, I find it very contradicting and full of dissonance, especially when coming from certain people who understand *action potential* and how it impacts human cognition, to *freely* ponder upon and argue in favor of the **non**existence of *free will*. Do you now see the irony in this belief? Even if, for the sake of argument, our brain decides before we become aware of it, it remains **our** brain after all, filled with all the built in biases mentioned in earlier chapters. Let us also recall the fact that reality as a whole is *confirmed information*, the subjectivity of which requires perceptive cognitive choice. Therefore, the choice of what is on the restaurant's menu happened within our being, and was affected by all that makes us who we are. In fact, many brilliant philosophers have addressed this issue based solely on observing behaviorism, conclusively saying: *"we are what we think"*. Hence, the events of our lives are there because we attract them there. I have seen the impact of changing my thinking system, and how the circumstances of my life drastically change as a direct result, sometimes based only on a slight alteration of the way I thought. As previously seen, even our emotions and feelings are choices of our intellect. Additionally, what does the concept of choice become without free will? On the flip side, what is the concept of free will without that of choice? Well, since we know for a fact that choice exists, the existence of free will also obviously becomes a fact. Indeed, believing in free will is compulsory. Otherwise, no human being would ever be culpable for anything he or she ever did; the murderer would not be blamed for deciding to kill your loved one(s) (god forbid), the thief would not be criticized for stealing your vehicle, and your own children would not be blamed for choosing to lie to you. Can you imagine the repercussions of such a meaningless life? One that would empower evil with the idea that there are no responsibilities to any action taken, due to the fact that there is no free will to begin with, and that it is all based on a primordial soup of utter randomness. Think about it, the hero would not be commended for risking his life to save another, the exam score at school would be meaningless, and your surgeon would **not** be an agent in performing your surgery. It would all just be... *happening*. You see how ridiculous this becomes upon scrutiny? If it is all just a random sequence of electricity in the brain that causes choices to be made, why is everything so coherent? For example, why is the artist capable of creating beautiful masterpieces? Why is Beethoven's music so beautiful? Well, Because of the notes he *chose*! Because he exercised that which is the privilege of human beings; our most beautiful and precious gift: *free will*. Since the connotation of our perceptions is subjective, and reality is *confirmed information*, it becomes undeniable that the choices we make conclusively shape the world. Hence, we have to be mindful of our choices... no matter how small.

* ~ * ~ * ~ * ~ * ~ * ~ * ~ * ~ *

Chapter 5

NOTHING IS NOTHING

G od is not found by atheists for the same reason that policemen are not found by thieves. Such is life; to each his own. In a debate entitled *God does not exist*, at the Oxford Union Society, atheist activist and former Christian preacher *Dan Barker* gave his arguments for his belief in the nonexistence of God. He said the following:

> *"If nothing comes from nothing, then God cannot exist, because God is not nothing. If that premise is true (that nothing comes from nothing) and if God is something, then you've just shot yourself in the foot."* **– Dan Barker**

This could not be further from the truth. In fact, I personally always found this argument funny. You see, since nothing comes from nothing, there could be no such thing as *nothing*, because we exist. Therefore, God **must** exist. In fact, the statement *nothing comes from nothing* is not strong enough. Rather, a more accurate statement is *nothing comes from nothing, on nothing, in nothing, with nothing, by nothing.* In order to understand my explanation of this, we must first cement in our thoughts that there is actually no such thing as **nothing**. The concept of nothing is only a notion that human beings use in order to explain the lack of something. For example, let us assume that I am searching for my keys and you tell me to look on the kitchen countertop. If I tell you: *I looked and found nothing,* you would understand that the kitchen countertop *lacks* my keys. But is there completely *nothing* there? This is the problem that atheists have. They fail to understand that there is no such thing as *nothing*. No matter how many entities of our existence we remove, we will always be left with **something** rather than **nothing**. Never will there be *nothing*. Allow me to elaborate even further with a simple exercise. What would be left if we start removing entities from our existence, one by one, until we have removed completely everything? Let us try...

Read the following → → →

Then close your eyes and imagine it before turning the page…

* * * * * * * * * * ***** * * * * * * * * * *

I have to admit that what you are about to do is not easy. It is actually an excerpt from an exercise I put together for mental stimulation, with the goal of increasing the amount of glial cells in the left parietal lobe, which would strengthen the process of synaptic activity in this technical area of the brain. Nonetheless, this watered-down version of the exercise can also be used to prove that there is no such thing as *nothing*. Are you ready? Here we go...

Look around you. What do you see? When I prompt you to close your eyes, start erasing these things one by one until the place you are in is completely vacant of everything you saw before closing your eyes. Erase everything! It is completely normal for it to seem too hard to do, or taking too long to accomplish. But stick to it, do not give up, and it will eventually start happening. The more you try, the more you will feel in control. It could help to practice removing only one thing, and then replacing it back a few times before removing more and more objects. I also advise you to do this exercise somewhere quiet, because the sounds you might hear will render the removal of entities around you that much harder.

Now look around, close your eyes, and erase everything before turning this page – and I mean **everything**. Nothing should be left!

Read the following → → →

Then close your eyes and imagine it before turning the page…

* * * * * * * * * * * ***** * * * * * * * * * *

Now that you have removed the entities present in your local vicinity, when I prompt you to close your eyes next, remove everything from the town or city you are currently in. Completely erase them from planet earth. For instance, if you are currently in Paris, you would remove the Eifel tower, the buildings, the streets, the parks, the people, etc., until nothing is left.

Close your eyes and erase your town before turning this page... Again, nothing should be left!

Read the following → → →

Then close your eyes and imagine it before turning the page…

* * * * * * * * * * ***** * * * * * * * * * *

Same as before, but this time remove everything from the country in which you currently are.

Close your eyes and erase the country before turning this page... Again, do not leave anything!

Read the following → → →

Then close your eyes and imagine it before turning the page…

* * * * * * * * * * ***** * * * * * * * * * *

Remove your continent.

You are doing great. Close your eyes…

Read the following → → →

Then close your eyes and imagine it before turning the page...

* * * * * * * * * * ***** * * * * * * * * * *

This time, when I prompt you to close your eyes, imagine that you are in outer space looking at planet earth.

Remove the planet.

Close your eyes…

Read the following → → →

Then close your eyes and imagine it before turning the page…

* * * * * * * * * * ***** * * * * * * * * * *

If you have been doing this properly, not only are you moving toward proof of the nonexistence of *nothing*, but you are also stimulating your brain for an increase in mental capabilities.

When I prompt you to close your eyes again, remove all other planets, as well as any other entity present in space, e.g., stars, asteroids, meteoroids, comets, and even the elements of our periodic table. Remove everything until space is completely empty; void of everything – even color.

Close your eyes...

For the following pages written in a bold font, only think about the question for some time before turning the page.

What are you left with?

* * * * * * * * * * * ***** * * * * * * * * * *

Nothing?

* * * * * * * * * * * ***** * * * * * * * * * *

No.

* * * * * * * * * * * * ***** * * * * * * * * * *

...you are left with empty space, and time.

* * * * * * * * * * ***** * * * * * * * * * *

That is not *nothing*...

* * * * * * * * * * **✳** * * * * * * * * * *

For example:

The following pages contain something...

* *

The previous pages lacked words, yes, but they still contained *something* rather than *nothing*. They contained space.

* * * * * * * * * * * ***** * * * * * * * * * *

Without space, this sentence could not exist!

* *

You are getting good at this, so…

* * * * * * * * * * ***** * * * * * * * * * *

Read the following → → →

Then close your eyes and imagine it before turning the page…

* * * * * * * * * * ***** * * * * * * * * *

We have reached a critical point in our little exercise. Now that nothing is left except *time* and *space*...

Close your eyes one last time and remove them as well.

Remove time and space before turning this page.

Go ahead, close your eyes...

For the following pages written in a bold font, only think about the question for some time before turning the page.

What are you left with now?

* * * * * * * * * * * ✱ * * * * * * * * * *

Nothing?

* * * * * * * * * * * ***** * * * * * * * * * *

No. But why?

* *

Well, because your consciousness exists!

You cannot erase that, can you?

* *

~~*~*~*~*~*~*~*

If at some point *nothing* existed, then how did everything that exists come into existence? In other words, if space is not there to contain it, and time is not there to set it in motion for creation, how could anything *happen*? And additionally, how can anything be, if there is no *consciousness* to incorporate it? In fact, if you were put in an empty room and asked to create something, but were given *nothing* to create anything with, you could not create anything with *nothing* even if you lived a thousand lifetimes. Could you? Of course not! And the reason is quite simple:

Nothing can come from nothing, on nothing, in nothing, with nothing, by nothing.

In order to further reinforce our understanding of the continual existence of something as opposed to nothing, and to also fully comprehend the fact that there is no such thing as *nothing*, we have to understand three types of situations:

- The first situation is ***possible existence***. You and I are a possible existence. We were born, but could have not been born. A baby could be born, but could also never be born at all. Rain might come down today, or might not come down for another week. The universe and everything in it exists, but could have not existed. These are all examples of what is known as *possible existence.*

- The second situation is ***forbidden existence.*** While you are sitting in your living room, can you also exist in your kitchen? Of course not! Can the planet Jupiter be found on the shore of a beach in Africa? No way! This is what is known as *forbidden existence.*

- The third and final situation is ***imperative existence***; God. Since we have established the fact that there is no such thing as nothing, the only imperative existence is that which has originated time, space, and everything else that exists, for the simple fact that *they exist.* The existence of a designer, originator, and creator is therefore ***imperative.*** God ***has*** to exist! Atheists argue, however, that if existence makes it imperative for a creator to exist, then who created God? They continue by asking *who created the God that created God.* And *who created the God that created the God that created God?* And their premise is that it is illogical because it would go on endlessly.

Take a look at what Barker said about this problem in the same debate mentioned earlier, which he said comes from Richard Dawkins' book *The Blind Watchmaker*:

> *"Anything that is complex enough to design a functional complexity, any deity who could design, has to have a mind that is at least as functionally complex as the thing that it designed. If your premise is that functional complexity requires a designer, if that's your premise, then the mind of that deity also must, by that premise, require a designer, and you get into this infinite regress of well then God needed a bigger God and a bigger God. I think most scientists prefer to just stop with what we do know rather than speculate endlessly about a mountain of turtles."* – **Dan Barker**

This argument brings us to a very crucial point. Considering the existence of God as imperative, and since God is not bound by space nor time, any intelligent person will conclude that God must not only exist, but also be eternal, which negates the absurd *infinite regress* argument mentioned here by Barker. I suspect that the problem he and his fellow atheists have is that it is hard for human beings to conceive of what I call an *eternal past*, i.e., the existence of God had no beginning. It is quite easy to conceive of an eternity in the future, for the simple reason that we are moving toward it. However, it is counter intuitive to conceive of something with no beginning because everything that exists, including the universe itself, had a beginning. Subsequently, since God is the creator of time, he is therefore not bound by it. God being completely independent from time renders the question of *"when did God start to exist?"* inapplicable. It would be like asking *"what is your favorite color of the alphabet?"* It would be plain silly! Understanding this concept is not *"a mountain of turtles,"* it is logic.

The Problem of Evil

The problem of evil, as some atheists put it, is the final argument I would like to address before moving on to proving the existence of God, as promised. Later in the debate, Barker said the following:

> *"All you have to do is walk into any children's hospital, and you know there's no God. At least no good God, maybe there's an evil God. Those children are dying at the same random rate, even though their parents are desperately praying, desperately loving those kids, wanting some kind of Divine intervention, and yet, as Ann Gaylor says, who is the former president of the freedom from religion foundation, nothing fails like prayer. That would be evidence! If you could give some scientific evidence that prayer actually makes an organic difference, not just makes you feel better, but an actual difference in the real world... that would be something to put on the table. The fact that that's not put on the table shows that prayer is pretty much talking to yourself. Finally, there is no need for a belief in God. Millions, tens of millions of people on this planet live happy lives, productive lives, moral lives, purposeful lives, lives of hope and meaning, without deluding ourselves that there are these invisible personalities populating some supernatural realm.*

We are quite happy, thank you, without that belief. Based on all of that, it is more likely to reject the proposition than to accept it. " – **Dan Barker**

To address *the problem of evil*, I have to elaborate on a very important aspect of our existence. Upon understanding the following statement, the dots will start to connect, and many profound questions that most of us ask ourselves pertaining to our existence will be answered:

That which you compare to infinity will always be zero.

Imagine the following hypothetical scenario: You are standing in an empty room with four walls and a ceiling. The room is ten feet wide and ten feet high. These two directions are, therefore, *finite*. Imagine the length, however, as *infinite*. You are standing five feet from the left wall and five feet from the right wall; in the middle, and your back is touching the wall behind you. You are looking forward, toward the *infinite* length of the room. Can you see the fourth wall ahead? Now remember, the room stretches infinitely in length. I suspect your answer to be that you do not see the wall because infinity is not measurable and extends *forever*. And this answer would be completely acceptable. However, for the sake of argument, imagine you start walking. You walk at four miles per hour for thirty three years nonstop. Can you **now** see the wall ahead? No, right? Because you are not any closer to it. But what if you start running? Imagine you run as fast as you can, without stopping, for seventy four years... you are still running... can you see the wall? No, because you are not any closer either. After having walked for thirty three years and ran as fast as you could for seventy four years, where are you in relation to the wall ahead? The math would look like this:

For walking:

    33 years

* 365 days / year

= 12,045 days of walking at a speed of 4 miles per hour. And...

    12,045 days

*   24 hours / day

= 289,080 hours of walking. And...

    289,080 hours

*   4 miles per hour

= 1,156,320 miles walked!

As for running:

    74 years

*   365 days / year

= 27,010 days of running at a speed of 15 miles per hour. And...

    27,010 days

*   24 hours / day

= 648,240 hours of running. And...

    648,240 hours

*   15 miles per hour

= **9,723,600 miles ran!**

Grand total traveled miles:

    1,156,320 miles of walking

+ 9,723,600 miles of running

= **10,879,920 miles**

You have traveled a total of 10,879,920 miles, which is roughly 450 times the circumference of the earth! Can you now see the wall?? A glimpse maybe? Far, far – far away? The answer is a solid **NO!** In fact, you are still not any closer to it at all. But what if, from the point you have reached so far, you get into a rocket ship that travels at the speed of light and *step on it* for 10,879,920 billion light years? Well, when you stop, your distance would still be *zero miles* in relation to the location of the wall at infinity. And what about the wall behind you? Well, your perpetual movement toward infinity would eventually make you even forget its existence. Which brings us to the realization that anything you compare to infinity becomes zero; nothing… utterly meaningless. The same concept is true when applied to time, i.e., that which you compare to **eternity** also becomes *insignificant*.

Our universe is finite; it had a beginning known as *the big bang*, and has an apparent end known as *the big crunch,* in which the distance of space eventually reverses, collapsing the universe to its extinction. However, the hereafter is eternal, which makes the world we currently live in completely *insignificant…*
Totally – absolutely – not – worthy – of – mention – *insignificant*. In fact, after eons upon eons upon eternally infinite eons of utmost infinite bliss in eternal heavens, no one will remember this current existence. It would become the forgotten antecedent of an eternal

life! If, after an eternity has passed, you were told that you lived a previous life of a measly one hundred years – and I say measly relative to eternity, of course – on a tiny little planet called earth, your answer would probably be:

No way?! Really?! ...Me?!

You would not remember it even if you were ill, poor, and tortured every single day of that life. It would basically be erased because of your ceaseless movement in time toward no apparent end.

Furthermore, paradise is different than our current life in many ways. There will be no pain, no famine, no illness, no sadness, and only an ultimate sense of euphoria during every second that passes. Hence, we realize that although God did not create evil, he simply allows it to exist because of the existence of eternity in the next life; the real and eternal one.

God also allows evil to exist because this life is nothing more than a system of trials:

*"Blessed is He [God] in whose hand is dominion, and He is over all things capable. **The one who created death and life***

to test you, as to which of you is best in deed, and He is The Honorable, The Forgiving." – **Qur'an 67:1, 2**

One of the very important things that Atheists fail to realize is that God is not only our maker, but also our proprietor, with complete authority over us. He is our master. God says:

"Has there come upon man a period of time when he was not a thing to even be mentioned? Indeed, We created man from a sperm mixture that We may try him; and We made him hearing and seeing. We guided him to the way, either he is thankful, or he is reprehensible."

– Qur'an 76:1 – 3

Was there a time when we did not exist? A time when we were not a thing to even be mentioned? Of course there was! Where were we before we existed? Therefore, anything we possess or receive, including our sheer existence, is a gift from God that we do not deserve. This is crucial to understand; that which we receive from God is not compensation, simply because it was not ours to begin with; it is a gift from God. An employee who does not receive his salary at the end of the week has the right to complain because he earned his money for the time he provided, i.e., fair compensation for his efforts. On the other hand, the provision of the master is considered a gift. Therefore, the ideology of a Muslim is that all the blessings that God bestows upon us, as well as anything that is averted from us, and even whatever is taken away from us after having *"owned it,"* was a gift we did not deserve to begin with. Hence, we cannot complain. As mentioned, even our outright existence belongs to God. A belief whence the popular Muslim expression comes: *"we belong to Allah and to him we shall return."*

But what happens when our faith is weak? What happens when we forget or ignore this reality? Imagine a parent drinking a cup of coffee. *"Dad, can I have a sip?"* his seven years old daughter tells him. The parent says, *"No, you can't"*. But, *"dad, please!"* she insists. He tells her, *"Ok, but just one sip, and you give it back"*. The child takes the cup and sips from it… twice. The parent says, *"Ok now give it back to me,"* but the child – hugging the cup with a smile – says, *"No, it's mine,"* forgetting that it was not hers to begin with! The same is true with us toward our creator. When he gives us we are overjoyed, and when he takes away we complain saying absurd things such as *"why me?"*, or *"what have I done to deserve this?"* If, as a Muslim with a strong faith in Allah, you incorporate intrinsically that nothing is yours to begin with, I do not fear for you; for you have taken the first step toward true happiness. You will be all right. God says:

"In order for you not to despair over that which eluded you, nor feel overjoyed in what came to you, and Allah does not like every self-deluded boastful." – **Qur'an 57:23**

Dan Barker said, *"All you have to do is walk into any children's hospital, and you know there's no God."* But he fails to understand that the current world these children live in is not the life they were created for. Considering these points, any sensible person will realize that it is actually God himself that will cure these children. He will give them everlasting life in ultimate bliss, which renders this current life, as well as their pain and suffering, obsolete. Come to think of it, it is Dan Barker's version of the *non-existence of God* that is evil. Because if God does not exist, these children's death would be the end of their story. Again, it all boils down to our perspective. Some people complain that God put thorns on roses. I praise and thank him for putting roses amongst thorns.

And because God exists, even if a person is ill for a thousand lives, it would still have zero significance because this world is finite and the next is eternal. But when you do not believe in life after death, and you think that this current life is all we have been created for, everything is dismantled and becomes seemingly evil. I tell you the opposite of what Barker said: *Based on all of that, it is more likely to **accept** the proposition than to reject it.*

Prophet Mohamad once explained to his companions that an angel will come to the people of heaven and give them each a letter from God. The letter will contain the following message:

From:

The Living Everlasting who does not die.

To:

The living everlasting who does not die.

I am the one who tells something to be and it is. Likewise, I now made you able to tell something to be and it becomes.

* ~ * ~ * ~ * ~ * ~ * ~ * ~ * ~ *

Chapter 6

FAITH IS BEYOND PROOF

The search for one's *self* requires the quieting of all mental noise. Amidst the restlessness and cacophony oozing from thoughts, opinions, and hopes, our reflection becomes obstructed. It is in silent contemplation – mental peace and quiet – that we understand ourselves. And when the peak of inner silence is reached, in this new found reticence, we actually find God. Undoubtedly, the search for one's self, if done for the sake of reaching virtue and beauty, ultimately leads to God. Trees, plants, and flowers grow in silence, and so does our faith in the one who created them and continues to provide sustenance also to our beating heart. The thumping sound it makes, however loud inside, is humbly silenced in search of the almighty force that set it in motion. And when the force is found, the heart of the believer becomes the throne of God. Some people, however, need proof...

SECTION 1:

Proving the Existence of God Logically

The existence of God is as discernable as the existence of human beings, for the simple fact that we exist and our world is governed by causality; a cause precedes every effect. If you see blocks of dominoes falling upon each other, you instinctively know that this is the effect, and the fact that there is a cause is not something you have to think about. There must have been a cause. Someone or something must have caused the tumbling of these dominoes. No doubt. Perhaps someone flicked the first one, or the wind pushed it, causing it to fall and create the chain reaction you saw. As such, every effect has its set of causes. But what if you only see the effect, and the cause is not directly perceivable with any of your five sense? Would this situation render the cause as non-existent? Of course not. And if a divine being presents himself as the cause for our existence, would he not be worthy of obedience and worship? Of course he would, even if he is not directly perceived with feeble means, which would not have the capacity to encapsulate his essence even if it tried. Let us dissect this reality further...

What would the terms *right* and *left* mean if there was no such concept as *right*? Would *left* still be *left*? How would we know *left* from *right* to begin with? In which case it would seem conceptually impossible to ascertain direction. For example, can you conceptualize a coin with only one side? When we first think of such questions, they seem totally impossible. However, if we were able to go *beyond the obvious* by diminishing the recognition process just enough; if we could temporarily forget what we know about the world we live in as well as its conventional inhibitions, we would have a clean slate to draw our imaginative concepts upon. After all, a genius perceives the universe as an unrestricted child who ponders upon his perceptions as if processing Aladdin's lamp. Let us dissect this subject even further...

We live in a world in which several dimensions exist. Some of which are known, but many have yet to be discovered. Take our spatial dimensions as an example. Zero dimension is basically nothing in space, and one dimension is a simple point of reference such as a location on a piece of paper. We would notice two dimensions if a dot or a line is drawn from that point on, and adding depth to the equation would have us enter the third dimension. The world we live in and interact with is *obviously* three dimensional, and any coin we think of, therefore, is going to be in three dimensions. Otherwise, it would not be a coin, but only a circle. Even if we draw a circle on a piece of paper and cut it out, we would still end up with a coin because it would inherit the depth of the piece of paper; 1 millimeter. Hence, two sides. Based on this, a question arises: How could we ever conceive of a coin with only one side, if the world we live in is three dimensional? Well, thereby lies the seed of faith in that which is not directly perceivable; faith in that which is *unseen*. Indeed, as human beings, it is imperative for us to believe in the unseen because our world teems with that which is invisible to our senses. Our previous understanding of the fact that there are no photoreceptors beyond the optic disc, for example, confirms that vision is conclusively *the beauty of seeing invisible things*; things such as love, for instance. Do you believe in love? I hope your answer is yes, in which case I would ask you to show it to me. Verily, it is when the unseen is felt that belief becomes manifest, sprouting with strength that turns it into conviction. Thus, in order to see proof of the existence of God, we have to first realize that there exists countless things that we cannot see, smell, feel, hear, nor touch, but can undoubtedly feel. Unfortunately, we live in a world brimming with palpable abstractions forcing us to cast some realities as *impossible.* If we constantly give into these inhibitions and move on carelessly, only because of a lack of tangibility, we would have ceded some of the most precious attributes of human life; hope, discovery, and true happiness.

* ~ * ~ * ~ * ~ * ~ * ~ * ~ * ~ *

The 2D Family and Their Triangles of Faith
The Story of an Unseen Dimension

Imagine a family of two dimensional beings living on a sphere. These two dimensional inhabitants have no knowledge that their world is three dimensional. They draw a small triangle on the face of their spherical world and, with keen intelligence, calculate that the sum of its angles is 180°. They soon realize that the angles of any triangle they draw have the same sum. However, as they draw larger and larger triangles, they reach a point when the lines start to curve around, taking the shape of the sphere they are drawn on; the triangle enters the third dimension. Thus, they are stumped to see that the sum of the angles of a very large *so called* triangle is more than 180°, due to the lines' curvature into the third dimension of their world. The two dimensional family notices the effect, but do not comprehend the cause because the third dimension is unknown to them. They do not possess an understanding of depth, nor height …yet. This is very logic since they live, view, and interact in only two dimensions. If they keep their wits about them, however, the family should start analyzing, theorizing, formulating, and finally reach an ultimate understanding of the third dimension, of which their entire world consists. The fourth dimension to us is exactly like the third dimension to them, i.e., unknown yet. This is only one example of things that are not directly perceived. What about the existence of God? Well, for us, God is akin to the third dimension for the 2D family. We sense his presence and know he exists, but cannot completely wrap our heads around the intricacies of his existence. Why? Because our feeble and finite mind does not have the capacity to incorporate the understanding of God's infinite scope. Indeed, the finite cannot directly perceive the infinite, but can nonetheless surely feel it. There was once an atheist teacher who always told his students that God did not exist because *"There is no evidence of design,"* he said. The students, wanting to prove him wrong logically, brought him a beautiful painting of a peacock as a gift. The painting made him happy. He smiled and said, *"Wow, that's beautiful! Who painted this?"* They all replied, *"no one did".* The teacher said, *"What do you mean? Is this a digital painting made by the computer?"* They said, *"Nope. Nothing was involved in the creation of this painting."* He said, *"This cannot be".* The students replied, *"Isn't that what you teach us? This is just a* **painting** *of a peacock, and you're already having a hard time believing that it just appeared from nothing. What about the* **real** *peacock... the feathers and the colors and the beautiful patterns?"* Knowing that a cause precedes every effect, the existence of God is proven by the simple fact that we exist. If anyone needs further logical proof for the existence of God, they need not look further than the mirror, where they will find conspicuous design; *the effect.*

SECTION 2:

Proving the Existence of God Mathematically

What is the largest number? Is it an octillion? No. A quindecillion? No, for the same obvious reason that it is not a googol, nor a googolplex. Is it infinity? Well, although it defines the unending array of cardinal numbers, infinity is not a number in and of itself. In fact, and for the sake of argument, the largest number is not even the infinite cardinal *Aleph Null* ($\aleph_0$) because of the transfinite ordinal *omega* (ω). How then do we answer this question? I asked myself the following: *since our entire existence and the universe containing it are finite, how can there be the presence of an unlimited amount of consistent numbers?* I wanted to satisfy my curiosity and provide closure to such an open ended reality. These questions peaked my interest in the subject. And no matter how elementary it seemed, I still pondered upon the fact that although we call our cardinal numbers *infinite*, the largest number has already been reached, acknowledged, used, and resides in some computer program somewhere, awaiting its successor to emerge. This new number would then, in turn, also be used in some algorithm or another, and this is where I had a problem. I could not accept the fact that this process would continue *only* until the expiration of time, space, and everything in it. My mind could not make sense of this because it meant that I belonged to a *finite* world with *infinite* attributes. How could that be? This reality seemed very weird to me. To resolve the issue, I had to create a world – in my mind's eye – in which the largest number could be reached and acknowledged; a number that would exist at infinity, but nonetheless be attainable. This proved to be very hard to do, and at times felt as though I was trying to fit an infinitely large elephant into a finite room with four walls and a ceiling. Thought after thought… I realized that our cardinal numbers are only *potentially* infinite, and to explain what exists beyond the big bang – if we traveled back in time – I had to create a unique concept. I came up with the concept of *absolute infinity*. Thinking retrospectively, I had to give my concept of *absolute infinity* a more contextual background, provide it with analytical value, and label it with an exclusively recursive categorical syntax for scientific analysis. Essentially, I invented a number which represents a concept, and this invention is my humble contribution to science:

AIOS (Pronounced: a-yoss)

$$(\infty)\overset{\circ}{1}$$

Absolute Infinite One Sukoon

Where the infinity symbol in between parenthesis represents "absolute infinity", and the circle above the 1 is the Arabic alphabetical symbol for rest (sukoon), which represents completion.

In my formula, two forms of infinity exist: *potential infinity*, which is a concept that we are accustomed to in our daily lives (such as how starting to count without stopping will never end; *potentially* going to ad infinitum), and *absolute infinity*, which is this new concept I created in order to explain a reality that is impossible for mere finite humans to experience. $(\infty)\overset{\text{o}}{1}$ AIOS is absolutely infinite.

For the naming convention, my reasoning was as follows: firstly, I used the infinity symbol to represent the infinite attribute of AIOS, but I also wrapped it in parenthesis in order to promote its unconditional and holistic completeness. Second, I used the number 1 digit because I realized that it is technically unattainable. Let me explain: from 1 derive all other numbers, i.e., the number 2 is a combination of two ones, and the number 3 a combination of three of them, etc. Notice how even floating point numbers are comprised of some fraction of 1. Hence, if we start from zero, keeping in mind that all numbers derive from 1, the number 1 itself becomes unattainable because it is infinitely divisible into partitions; namely, 0.1, 0.2, 0.3, etc. This is the reason why I concluded that the digit that should be used to explain a *state of* AIOS is 1. And since AIOS is *absolutely infinite*, i.e., it is whole and complete as much as it is infinite, I chose to represent this concept with the *sukoon* (^{o}): $\overset{\text{o}}{1}$. Hence, I named it *one sukoon*. And there you have it: **Absolute Infinite One Sukoon.**

Again, this was very hard for me to formulize, as it proved to be an unfamiliar concept; a very peculiar concept. The more I reflected, however, the more I was able to envision it, and the following analogy finally made it clear in my mind:

$$0.9999... = 1$$

* ~ * ~ * ~ * ~ * ~ * ~ * ~ * ~ *

AIOS is a state. It is the name of a capacity that is infinite, but nonetheless complete. As such, it encompasses the universe and everything in it including space, time, and our consciousness. As a result, questions containing words such as *when* or *where* do not apply to it. AIOS is not simply in a completely different category, but actually encompasses all that is categorical. The big bang, time, space, the expanding universe, as well as our cardinal numbers are neither infinite, nor are they complete, but simply perpetually itemized within a greater whole until it expires. This greater whole is encompassed by AIOS; *an environment with no beginning, nor end:*

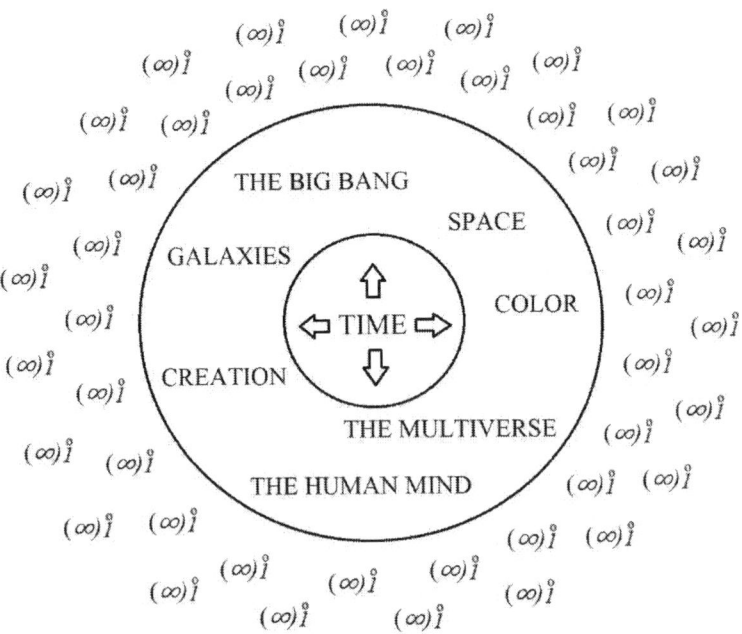

Since time had a beginning, what existed before? In other words, what does AIOS *look* like? To fully understand what lies beyond the *circle* of creation, we must once more detach from conventional inhibitions. That which lies beyond remained unfamiliar to me, even long after my discovery of it. What we perceive is labeled, and that label is a chain holding us back; it is stopping us from reaching outside what seems obvious.

In 1927, British astronomer *Arthur Eddington* proposed a theory that showed time moving in only one direction; *the arrow of time*. His proposal suggests that the past and the future are asymmetrical. *"If as we follow the arrow we find more and more of the random element in the state of the world, then the arrow is pointing towards the future,"* Eddington explained. He came to this conclusion by studying the organization of atoms and molecules based on the flow of time. What I find very interesting – and relevant to our subject – is that he further entertains three important notions about this *arrow,* the first of which I would like to mention here. He says: *"It is vividly recognized by consciousness".* This is the statement that made me ponder, and eventually realize, that time does not strictly follow a *single direction* causing the past and the future to be asymmetrical, as proposed by Eddington. If it did, it would imply that as a dynamical system, our experiences are always happening in the past. Why? Well, because of the interim caused by the transduction process; the time it takes our experiences to arrive at our monitoring consciousness. Remember? Our senses are only messengers and, therefore, these breaks in time would be at the intervals when the observer is experiencing, conceptualizing, or recognizing a particular point in time. This is a flawed notion in my opinion, not only because time cannot be stopped nor foreshadowed, but also because this concept would negate the sustenance of energy and matter; it would contradict entropy. Think about it for a moment... if time is constantly ahead of us, it took the world with it, did it not? If time flows in one direction asymmetrically, and consciousness – being a fundamental entity involved – is lagging behind, then what provides confirmation for our experiences? Even worse, what confirms our sheer existence? My theory suggests that the past and the future are both one and the same. It will seem as an unfamiliar conception, but I suggest that as opposed to moving in a single direction, time is holistically flowing around us like a ripple in still water. The past and the future are both different manifestations of the same thing. Confusing? Let me ask you this: *since we are constantly moving from the past to the future, **when** is the present?* Well, based on my theory, never. Because as soon as you say **now**, that instance has already past. Therefore, we are at all times *all the time*, and this is where AIOS comes in: a concept showing what lies beyond; beyond space, beyond time... beyond our consciousness.

* ~ * ~ * ~ * ~ * ~ * ~ * ~ * ~ *

God is AIOSal

Because AIOS is the name of a state with a capacity that is holistically infinite but nonetheless complete, I was able to put together a formula that shows what existed before time; before the big bang.

Let e be a measurable set representing *existence*...

...and t be a measurable set representing *time*.

$$(\infty)\overset{o}{1} = e - t \therefore (t=0) = (\infty)\overset{o}{1}$$

Time is encompassed in a state of AIOS; in a state of infinite capacity that is also complete. E*xistence* has to have been AIOSal (Unbound by time) because AIOS, as opposed to time which is finite, is *absolutely infinite* $((\infty))$. Hence, $e - t$ (existence minus time) renders $t=0$ to be equal to $(\infty)\overset{o}{1}$, i.e., the initial setting before the big bang could not have been *nothing*, because of the state of AIOS having to exist in order to encompass everything else. Thus, there has never been a time when *nothing* existed because time itself has not always existed to begin with. How can anyone say that there was a **time** when nothing existed, since **time** itself had a beginning? But if we travel back to before the presence of time and reach the edge of AIOS, we know that there could **not** have been *0* because $(\infty)\overset{o}{1}$ exists. In other words, if starting from zero, it would take an infinite percentage of time to holistically reach 1 (creation) because division by *0* is undefined:

$$1 / 0.1 = 10$$
$$1 / 0.01 = 100$$
$$1 / 0.001 = 1,000$$
$$1 / 0.0001 = 10,000$$

Etc.

As we can see, when we divide by 0, the closer the denominator is to zero the larger the result becomes. So, does division by zero equal infinity? No, because the same thing happens (although in the negative) even when we divide by negative numbers:

$$1 / -0.1 = -10$$
$$1 / -0.01 = -100$$
$$1 / -0.001 = -1,000$$
$$1 / -0.0001 = -10,000$$

Etc.

Again, the closer we are to zero, the larger the negative result becomes toward *negative infinity*, which is a very different outcome than *positive infinity*.

Finally, trying to define *0* with:

$$0/0$$

(zero divided by zero)

…is as empty as it sounds, void of any substance and even rendering the concept insignificant.

You now might be thinking: *could division by zero be equal to* $(\infty)\overset{o}{1}?$ The answer is also *no* because infinity is involved here as well. Hence, division by zero remains undefined.

In light of this, even if we turn around and realistically surf the wave of time in the opposite direction, further and further into the past until we have moved beyond everything in existence including space, time, and *color*, we would still find something which has always existed; something AIOSal because division by 0 is null…

And so it is that $(\infty)\overset{o}{1} = e - t$ mathematically proves that before time and space, before the existence of our universe and everything in it, there has always been something; ***There has always been God*** *in a state of **imperative existence**;* in a state that is AIOSal!

* ~ * ~ * ~ * ~ * ~ * ~ * ~ * ~ *

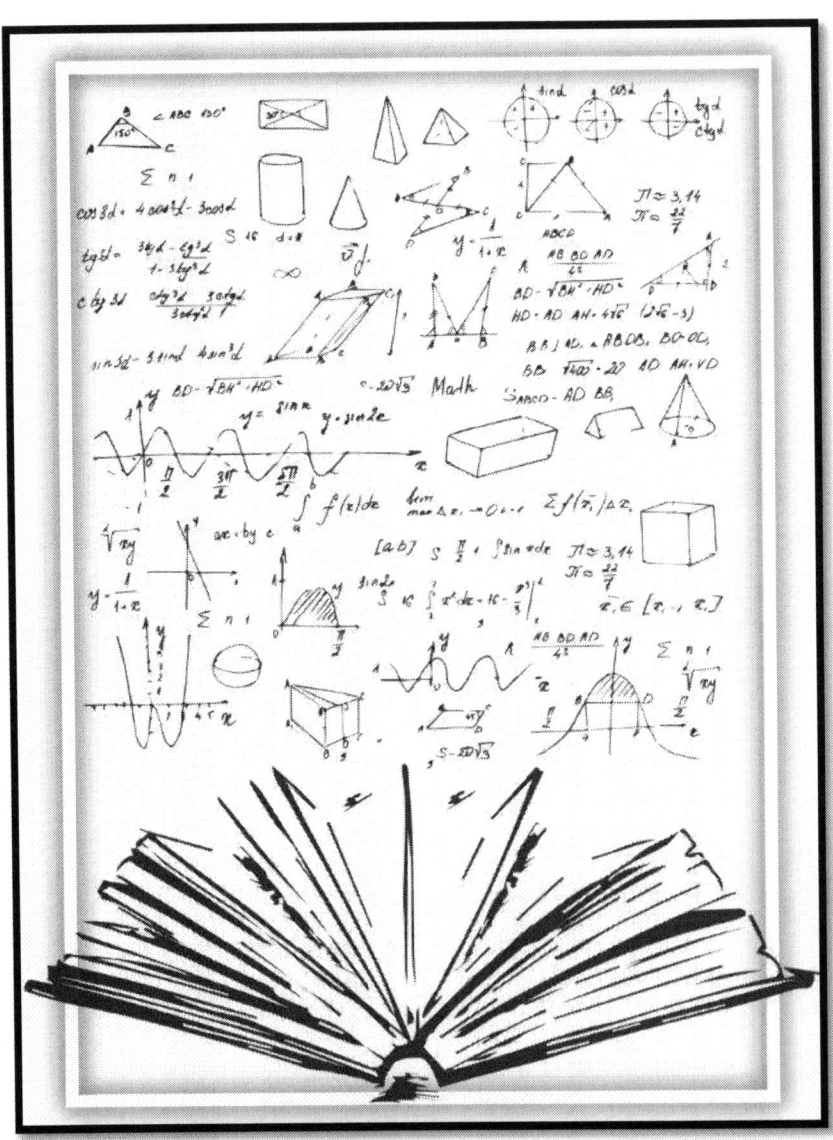

SECTION 3:

Proving the Existence of God Scientifically

Many of the confirmed philosophical and scientific ideas recently discovered were already mentioned in the Qur'an. God says:

> *"We have made available for people in this Qur'an from every example..."* **– Qur'an 17:89**

One of these examples involves the expansion of space. It is said that the astronomer *Edwin Hubble* discovered, using the Hooker telescope at Mount Wilson Observatory, that space is expanding. Hubble's proposition – that galaxies were further away from each other every time he looked at them – became proof for the expansion of space. Surprisingly, I found that another astronomer by the name of *George Lemaitre* had actually discovered this interesting situation of the universe *before* Edwin Hubble. However, the discovery was named *Hubble's Law* because, although George Lemaitre had published the same work, Hubble had published it in a more visible journal. I read this and smiled, because over one thousand four hundred years earlier, the holy prophet of Islam, Mohamad, without the use of a sophisticated telescope – or any telescope for that matter – came with a verse from the Qur'an which says:

*"And the heaven We have created with hands and **We are expanding it."** – **Qur'an 51:47**

I tell you: There is no journal, nor book, that is more *visible* than the Qur'an. Therefore, if it is a matter of how visible a journal is, then this discovery should be named **Prophet Mohamad's law**!

This is already scientific proof, before even going any further, that the Qur'an is the word of God. Science actually completely agrees with approximately three quarters of this holy book, and the other quarter is only ambiguous; science does not necessarily confirm it yet, but it does not contradict it either. Take a look at other examples of fairly recent discoveries which were all mentioned in the Qur'an over fourteen hundred years earlier:

The big bang:

"Have those who disbelieved not considered that the heavens and the earth were a joined entity, and We rendered them asunder..."

– Qur'an 21:30

~~*~*~*

Nebulae (where stars are born) look like the painting of a flower when their image is captured after a supernova explosion:

"And if the heaven is split, it was like a flower, like paint."

– Qur'an 55:37

~~*~*~*

Life was created from water:

"...and We made from water every living thing. Will they not believe?" **– Qur'an 21:30**

~~*~*~*

The crystallization of water:

The crystallization of water has, fairly recently, been scientifically shown by *Dr. Masaru Emoto* to change based on varying sound vibrations. Dr. Emoto collected samples of water from several different sources, and froze the specimens in order to study them under the microscope of his laboratory. Emoto and his staff also observed the frozen water specimens after exposing them to music and prayer. Dr. Emoto wrote, *"It was 1994 when the idea to freeze water and observe it with a microscope came upon me. With this method, I was convinced that I should be able to see something like snow crystals,"* He continued, *"The result was that we always observed beautiful crystals after giving good words, playing good music, and showing, playing, or offering pure prayer to water. On the other hand, we observed disfigured crystals in the opposite situation. Moreover, we never observed identical crystals. I published these results as photograph collections: Messages from Water 1 (1999), Messages from Water 2 (2002), Messages from Water 3 (2004), and Messages from Water 4 (2008). (All of them are published from Hado Kyoiku-Sha)".*

I recognized that this is one of the reasons why certain types of music are forbidden in Islam. As a Muslim, one must understand the importance of knowing human anatomy, such as the fact that 65% of our bodies are made of water. Also, since ears are a direct pathway to the heart, it ultimately becomes the source of actions. Let me explain... Imagine someone yelling at you, but his voice is muted; you cannot hear him. His yelling would not affect you much, even if you can see him. At worse, it might seem very weird to see someone yelling at the top of his lungs without any sound emerging from his mouth. At best, it might just be plain funny. However, actually hearing the screams would undoubtedly cause some change in your emotions, even without seeing the person. When looking at the entertainment/music industry today, we realize how much effect it has on human hearts, and how evil it has become. I understood this. Therefore, as soon as I hear music that might *change the crystallization of the water in my body to my detriment*, I close *the pathway to my heart*; I close my ears. If for nothing else, as seen earlier, out of the mere principle that what we sense with our five senses is what we get, but it might not be all that there is.

The discovery of the change in the crystallization of water based on sounds and words further proves the prophethood of Prophet Mohamad, as well as the validity of his message. You see, the prophet advised his followers to speak the words *"in the name of God the compassionate the merciful"* aloud on water before drinking, at a time when the technology needed to know such facts was nonexistent. This, to me, is clear proof that this simple but effective advice cannot be from other than divine origin.

~~*~*~*

Freshwater and seawater meet but do not mix:

> *"He made the two seas meet. Between them is a transitional barrier; they do not transgress. So which of the favors of your Lord will you deny?"* – **Qur'an 55:19 – 21**

Indeed, although there is no actual barrier separating freshwater and sea water when they meet, they are nonetheless intersected by a clearly dividing line.

~~*~*~*

Qur'anic precision:

The following shows two instances of the definite precision of the Qur'an. One concerning spiders, and the other concerning bees. You will appreciate this precision even more if you keep in consideration the fact that the Qur'an was revealed over a period of approximately twenty years. Surely, if this book was from human origin, you would have found in it many discrepancies and contradictions, due to the length of time that passed between each verse, section, or chapter revealed. But this is not the case. It is actually quite the contrary. We see precise distinction even between the gender of tiny little insects such as spiders and bees. For example, although both male and female spiders can produce silk and create webs, arachnology tells us that adult male spiders build webs only for courting and sperm induction. Female spiders, on the other hand, not only build more significant and complicated webs, but also live around them; they take them as homes. Therefore, the next time you see a spider living on a web, know that it is more likely to be a female. Interestingly enough, take a look at the precision by which the Qur'an gives the following analogy:

> *"The example of those who take trustees other than Allah, is like the example of a spider taking for **herself** a home. And the weakest of homes is the home of the spider, if only they knew."* – **Qur'an 29:41**

Furthermore, it was discovered also fairly recently that worker bees; the ones that gather pollen and make honey, are all females. However, this was actually hinted to in the Qur'an, more than one thousand four hundred years ago in the following verses:

> *"And your lord inspired the bees to 'take* [the Arabic word used here for **take** is **'ettakhedhee'**, which addresses her in the **feminine**] *for yourself houses among the mountains, and among the trees, and in that which they construct. Then eat from all fruits, and follow the ways your lord has laid for you.' From **her** bellies emerges a drink, varying in color, in which there is healing for people. In that is a sign for a people who reflect."* – **Qur'an 16:68, 69**

~~*~*~*

The human embryo:

> *"And We have created man from an extract of clay, and made it into sperm into a robust womb, and made the sperm into a clot, then made the clot into a lump, then made the lump into bones, and dressed the bones with flesh, then we raised it as a different creation. So revered is Allah the best of creators."* – **Qur'an 23:12 – 14**

It was only recently that we discovered how the embryo latches onto the mother to feed, and how it develops from there. Scientific research has shown that, as mentioned in the Qur'anic verses above, the sperm transforms into a clot, which turns into a lump, from which point bones appear to, only then, be dressed with flesh and muscle. I ask you, dear reader, if it was not from Divine revelation, how could have Prophet Mohamad known this precise order of formation as early as one thousand four hundred years ago?

~~*~*~*

The multiverse and dark matter:

> *"Exalted is He in whose hand is power, and He is over all things capable. He created death and life to burden you as to which of you is best in deed, and He is The Honorable, The Forgiving.* **He created seven heavens in layers.** *You will not see in the creation of The Merciful any inconsistencies.* **So redirect your sight: do you see any disequilibrium? Then return your sight twice again. Your vision will return to you in defeat and regret.** *And We adorned the sky of this world with lanterns..."*

> **– Qur'an 67:1 – 5**

In 2001, NASA launched a probe into space called The Wilkinson Microwave Anisotropy Probe (WMAP). With the help of the information it was able to gather, scientists mapped the conditions as they existed in the early universe after the big bang, showing a pattern of tiny fluctuations in the Cosmic Microwave Background radiation, i.e., the oldest light in the universe. But scientists are now speculating that our universe is actually one of many; that our universe is part of a multiverse. You see, astronomers and physicists have recently confirmed the existence of dark matter, a mysterious energy present in space acting as one of the building blocks of the multiverse, and making up approximately 75 to 80% of the mass of our known universe. Suddenly, an entire generation of text books have to be thrown out. Indeed, our science teachers were wrong when they said, *"the universe is only made up of atoms"*. Although dark matter is invisible to us, we can detect its gravity, which is how we know it exists. Light passing through a galaxy causes a gravitational field to be generated, bending it as a result, i.e., the light is distorted. This reality is called *gravitational lensing*, and was predicted by Albert Einstein in his work on general relativity. Although dark matter does not emit any light, we can still locate it using gravitational lensing. When light bends in odd places, we know the reason for it: the presence of a mysterious energy: dark matter. In order to evaluate certain attributes of the dark matter bending the light, we had to first look to trace the light emitted from galaxies in the background, and then look again to establish not only its distance, but also the angle of lensing. Hence, the first time we looked at the emitted light, we saw distortion and discrepancy, i.e., *disequilibrium* because of *the bend*. I propose that if we entertain the idea that dark matter is intertwined in several universes, we realize what God is saying regarding the superimposed seven heavens: *"He created seven heavens in layers... So redirect your sight; do you see any disequilibrium? Then return your sight twice again; your vision will return to you in defeat and regret."* I ask you, dear reader, if it was not from Divine revelation, how could have Prophet Mohamad known the intricate interference which dark matter creates, as far back as a millennia and a half ago? I tell you, there was no probe launched from Mecca nor Medina to observe tiny fluctuations in the Cosmic Microwave Background radiation, nor was there any gravitational lensing technology available. Yet again, we see no *disequilibrium* in the verses of the Holy Qur'an. Proof of pure revelation from a Divine, all wise, all knowing creator.

~~*~*~*

What is smaller than an atom?

"And those who disbelieved said 'the hour will not come to us'. Say [O Mohamad]*: yes by my Lord, it will surely come to you, The One* [God] *that knows of the unseen does not escape from His knowledge even the weight of **an atom** in the heavens or within the earth, **nor that which is smaller**, nor larger. All is recorded in an evident book."*

– Qur'an 34:3

In this verse, we see a mention of the atom in the Qur'an, but what is even more interesting is the mention of *that which is smaller*. Considering that *the hour* mentioned in the verse is in reference to the day of judgement, take a look at another verse also mentioning this day. This time, however, we are given a hint about *that which is smaller* than an atom:

> *"The day We summon every group and their leader. Then whoever is given his book in his right hand, these people will read their book, and will not be oppressed even* **as little as a string.**" – **Qur'an 17:71**

Since the context of these verses is the same, it ill behooves to understand *that which is smaller than an atom*, as something other than what is popularly known today in the scientific world as *String Theory*; a cutting edge theoretical framework, proposing one dimensional objects called strings to be the building blocks of everything in existence – *smaller than an atom*.

Indeed, God says:

> *"We will show them Our signs in the horizons* [dark matter & gravitational lensing for example] *and within themselves* [atoms & strings for example] *until it becomes evident to*

them that it is the truth. But is it not sufficient concerning your Lord, for Him to be over all things a witness?"

– Qur'an 41:53

~~*~*~*

In light of all this, it would be completely logic to say that if science shows the accuracy of approximately three quarters of the Qur'an, by being in complete accord with the information contained therein, the other quarter – which has not yet been confirmed – **must** also be correct! In which case this holy book is clearly from a divine, all knowing, almighty creator.

Although science has provided indispensable information, it can only tell us how to **do** things. The Qur'an, on the other hand, entices us to research and learn through science while providing not only the foundation for reaching perfect scientific principles, but also the necessary components for true enlightenment:

The direct developmental procedures for the perfection of morals.

* ~ * ~ * ~ * ~ * ~ * ~ * ~ * ~ *

~ PART THREE ~

A STUDY IN JUXTAPOSITION

Searching for the truth – finding it.

The truth is upon us. We just have to iron out the coiling. This part of the book is unusual. For starters, I chose to compare only Christianity to Islam, in order to keep it simple, but expect that the comparison process to any other religious order of the world will be the same.

In Part three here, I defend the prophets, especially the last of them: Prophet Mohamad. I offer clear confirmation of his truthfulness and trustworthiness. The final chapter will actually reveal an echo that originated from the pinnacle of greatness and virtue; a perfect representation of the truth in all its beauty!

Now that the painting has been dusted off, refurbished, and restored to its initial allure – thanks to that which came before – let us take a few steps back and gaze upon its entire beauty – unshackled.

Go on... flip the pages and notice how our synapses are not only a manifestation of who we are, but also the gardens of fate. We will see the importance of being aware of what we sow in them with our actions and deeds. And, even more importantly, we will confirm our beliefs, and substantiate our allegiances.

"Do you not see that Allah has made subject to you whatever is in the heavens and whatever is on earth, and bestowed upon you His blessings; apparent and ulterior? And of the people is he who argues about God without knowledge, nor guidance, nor an enlightening Book. And when it is said to them 'Follow what Allah has revealed', they say, 'Rather, we will follow that which we found our fathers following'. Is not Satan inviting them to a punishment in hellfire?"

– Qur'an 31:20, 21

Chapter 7

OFTEN UNDISCLOSED

Compassionate and beneficent, God enlightens the path of those who seek the truth. There are some, however, that refuse to accept it, blind and heedless of the facts laid down before them.

It was a clear and sunny day, our backyard's grass was freshly cut, and it felt like the perfect time to play catch with the kids. As I threw the baseball to my son, I saw two people standing at the front gate. One of them was carrying a big brown bag, so I figured that they came to preach. There was an older man in his sixties and a younger one in his twenties. I walked toward them and said, *"good morning! Can I help you?"* The older man replied, *"We've come to talk to you about how Jesus died for you, as well as the way to heaven."*

I said, *"Sure, I love Jesus! Let's sit on the porch. My name is ▓▓▓▓,* *what are your names?"*

The older man said, *"I'm Tom"*, and the younger one, *"Ben."*

I replied, *"Nice to meet you both!"*

As we all sat down, Tom looked at me and said:

> *"Did you know that if you lived a perfect life but only committed one lie, God would* **have to** *put you in hell?"*

I said, *"So you're saying that God does not have the capacity to forgive? What about God's mercy?"*

> Tom replied, *"God had to make a way... so he sent his son as a man in the flesh to die for our sins."*

I said, *"But there's a problem with that..."*

> Inquisitive, Tom asked, *"Really? What is it?"*

I replied, *"The death of* **a man** *cannot possibly pay for the sins of the whole world, can it? He had to die as* **a God!***"*

> Tom said, *"He did die as a God!"*

I continued, *"And having died as* **a God***, did Jesus pay the full price for our sins?"*

> He replied, *"Yes of course!"*

So I quickly asked, *"Then why is there a day of judgement?"*

There was silence for a few seconds. In fact, no reply ever came. Instead, he looked at my son and said:

"Your dad is a very intelligent man!"

I said, *"Thank you, but please answer. If I pay full price for something you have, can you claim any right to that something afterward?"*

He said, *"Yes I can! If you sign a contract."*

I told him, *"A contract? Although having paid full price? And you think that's fair?"*

Seemingly confused, Tom said, *"This is beside the point, Jesus was the son of God sent down as a man in the flesh. You wouldn't be able to tell he was God."*

I replied, *"You lost me here... so is he God or not?"*

He said, *"He is the **son** of God!"*

I said, *"Yes but do you consider him to be God in the flesh?"*

He said, *"He is God incarnate!"*

I asked, *"And the Holy Ghost?"*

Tom, *"God!"*

I asked, *"Mr. Tom, Please explain to me how 3 can be 1 together at the same time?"*

He paused and looked at the floor. After a few seconds he finally said:

"It's beyond me... that's what the scriptures say."

I further asked, *"Did Jesus say?"*

"Say what?" He said – again seemingly lost.

"That he is God," I said firmly. I continued, *"find me one simple explicit statement in your bible from the lips of Jesus saying: "I am God!"*

Tom said, *"He said it all the time!"*

I said, *"Find only one! That's all it would take to convince me."*

Tom started flipping the pages. I could tell he was nervous, but although I felt bad for him, I had to make a point. He then looked at his young follower, Ben, and said:

"Don't you have a Bible? Can't you help?"

Ben, without opening his bible, surprised us by suddenly saying:

"I and the father are one."

To his credit, I thought that was beautiful. I smiled and said:

*"Jesus did say that in John 10:30. However, you cannot take this verse and interpret it out of its context. Ben, my brother, please read the verses that precede this one and you will realize the actual context; understanding what the verse means. Namely, that Jesus and the Father are one **in purpose**."*

As I spoke to Ben, Tom interrupted and started reading John 8:58:

> *"Jesus said unto them, verily, verily, I say unto you, Before Abraham was, I am."*

I said…

*"Again, look at the context by reading the verses that came before this one! I AM is the name of God **the father**, mentioned in other passages of the bible as well, and Jesus explains this clearly in the verses leading to verse 58. Besides, is this even Jesus speaking? Or is this the gospel of John? As in, is the Bible that Christians around the world possess today a book that Jesus wrote as a scripture revealed by God, or to be called a book of his own?"*

Tom said, *"Why are you doing this?"*

I replied *"I'm only asking simple questions…"*

* ~ * ~ * ~ * ~ * ~ * ~ * ~ * ~ *

Naturally, one of the very first questions that arise, when doing such a comparative study of beliefs, is whether or not the book of a particular religion is indeed a heavenly one. This question is vitally important. And as far as the Bible is concerned, although still containing some of the truth, I have confirmed that the original teachings of Jesus have been altered with many added fabrications and interpolations. In order to investigate this aspect, I began by asking myself the following simple questions:

Is the Bible that Christians around the world possess today a book that Jesus wrote himself, making him the author?

The answer was clear: **No.**

Did Jesus request from anyone, or even simply desire for someone at any time during his life, to write anything on his behalf?

No.

Was the Bible that Christians possess today written during the time of Jesus?

No.

Was it written immediately after the departure of Jesus?

No.

Indeed, the answers to these questions gave me confirmation for what the Christian Literature Society, *Madras*, reveals in the book *The Founder of Christianity and His Religion* on page 17 where it says, *"The whole Bible contains sixty six books written by forty different authors over a space of about fifteen centuries."* Moreover, the book also says, *"Jesus himself wrote nothing. Oral teaching was for several years – the only means employed in the spread of Christianity. It was for the guidance of the young converts that the earliest writings of the New Testament were composed."* The same book further discloses, *"They were probably written about twenty years after the death of Christ".* Furthermore, it states on page 18, *"The gospels do not give a complete history of the life of Christ, they are rather memoirs."*

In fact, if the Bible is the word of God inspired and written by the disciples of Jesus, how would the differences in the Books be explained? For example, the Douay-Rheims Catholic version of the Bible contains books which the Protestant version does not. Why? The omitted books are as follows:

The Book of Tobias
The Book of Judith
The Book of Wisdom
The Book of Ecclesiasticus

The Book of Baruch

The Book of 1 Maccabees

The Book of 2 Maccabees

Mr. Benjamin Wilson, in his introduction to the *Emphatic Diaglott*, published by the *Watch Tower Society* and containing the original Greek text of what is commonly known as *The New Testament*, mentions the following facts:

"King James Bible, or the Authorized Version, was published in 1611. In the year 1604, forty-seven persons learned in the languages were appointed to revise the translation then in use. They were ordered to use the Bishop's Bible as the basis of the new version, and to alter it as little as the original would allow; but if the prior translations of Tyndale, Coverdale, Matthew, Cranmer or Whitechurch, and the Geneva editors agreed better with the text, to adopt the same. This translation was perhaps the best that could be made at the time, and if it had not been published by kingly authority, it would not now be venerated by English and American Protestants, as though it had come direct from God. It has been convicted of containing over 20,000 errors. Nearly 700 Greek MSS. are now known, and some of them very ancient; whereas the translators of the

common version had only the advantage of some 8 MSS. none of which was earlier than the tenth century."

Hence, I concluded that most of what is mentioned in the Bible is not the truth. However, some of the teachings of Jesus did find their way into the book nonetheless. As a result, some verses of the Bible do reveal the truth and, as we will soon see, actually direct toward Islam.

Can God Die?

Christianity is established on the doctrine of atonement, i.e., *Jesus died for our sins.* This is the foundation of the religion. I impartially studied this concept in order to compare and contrast and fully give Christianity a chance. I wanted to hold a belief of my own understanding and research. At first, I actually found the idea of *a redeemer* to be very attractive, perhaps because it is part of human nature to possess the will to be saved. It seemed like a nice and comforting solution. Yet, I soon realized that in order to embrace Christianity based on this concept, I would have to blindly follow its teachings without further questioning the trinity. I was even told that the trinity will not make sense to mere mortal humans. Therefore, it seemed completely counter intuitive to be *saved* merely by accepting Jesus in my heart and acknowledging that he freed me from my sins, without understanding *what* God is. Indeed, the doctrine of atonement dictates that no one can ever be righteous; we have all been created as sinners, and the only way to heaven is through the redeemer: *Jesus Christ.*

It is this *doctrine of atonement,* on which the entirety of Christianity is based, that caused problems for me. I asked myself: *why does God **need** to physically beget a son to pay for our sins? God is the omnipotent, almighty creator of everything in existence... is he not?*

If God wants to punish... he punishes, and if he wants to forgive...
he forgives! Who in the universe has the authority to adjudicate him
anyway?

Besides, when you pay full price for something, that *thing* becomes
your own, and the previous owner forfeits all his claims for the price
he has received. I evaluated: *if the sins of man have been paid for,*
why do Christians have a day of Judgement? If that's the premise,
then God has no right to punish or even judge any sinner. With that
presumption, people are free to do anything they want because God
undoubtedly met the cost of all sins. This is confirmed by the
following verse of the bible, which basically states that all we need
to be redeemed is a belief in Jesus:

John 3:16
"For God so loved the world that he gave his only begotten
Son, that whosoever believeth in him should not perish, but
have everlasting life. "

I reflected: *can this ever be sensible logic or common sense? Why*
would God not just forgive all our sins if that's what he wants? Why
does he have to kill the person he loves most in order to forgive us?
It did not make any sense to me. In fact, the more I thought about

it, the more I realized that if somebody has to die for someone else to be forgiven, there is actually no forgiveness. Killing someone in order to forgive another means taking the price and exacting the full sanction, which is what a callous judge would do. On the other hand, if God is *loving and kind* as mentioned in the Bible, then why would he not save his son? The irony is that the Bible also mentions that the son was not even willing, and was actually seeking deliverance from the imminent crucifixion. Take a look:

Matthew 27:45

*"And about the ninth hour Jesus cried with a loud voice, saying, **Eli, Eli, lama sabachthani?** (My God, my God, why hast thou forsaken me?)"*

I further thought that if the son loves the people so much as to die for them, does not the father love the people more than the son loves them? Of course he does! Why then does the father refrain from dying himself for the sins of people? Who would kill their son in order to save somebody else? Certainly not almighty God! As far as I am concerned, I would sacrifice myself to protect not only the stranger in the process, but more importantly my son. Some Christians say that it **was** God himself that died on the cross. But this caused even more problems for me because it would mean that if a sin is committed, it cannot be forgiven until the lord sacrifices himself. That would be absurd because if God wanted to forgive me, could he not simply do it? Why does he have to pay for sins in order to forgive them? And if the father condemns you, but the son wants to save you, how can they both be one and the same? I asked and asked… yet no answer came.

Is Jesus God?

The divinity of Jesus is the major difference between Christianity and Islam. During my research, I could not accept that Jesus is God for the simple fact that he never claimed to be God, nor did he ever say *worship me*. I could not find a single unequivocal statement in any of the 66 books of the Bible – or the 73 of the Roman Catholics – where Jesus says *I am God* or *worship me*. From the lips of Jesus, I could not find even one simple straightforward explicit statement indicating such will. In light of this, I started thinking: *miraculous birth? Yes! Messiah? Yes! Gave life to the dead and cured the blind and the leper? Yes!* Muslims even accept the term *Son of God*, as long as it is taken as *he who has received life from God*. I further discovered that when the concept of *sonship* is used in the bible, it is actually only to mean *he who has received life from god*. My first confirmation came when I read that Jesus is addressed as the son of man. Take a look:

> **Luke 7:34**
>
> *"The **son of man** is come eating and drinking and ye say, behold a glutinous man, and a wine bibber, a friend of publicans and sinners."*

Luke 9:26

*"For whosoever shall be ashamed of me and of my words, of him shall the **son of man** be ashamed, when he shall come in his own glory, and in his Father's, and of the holy angels."*

I also discovered that, although Jesus did address God as his father, he also addressed him as **our** father. This means that God is taken as **our** father – our creator – as much as the father of Jesus – his creator. Hence, it became clear to me that Jesus' son-ship should be taken in the sense of *a creature of God*. The term *son of God*, used by Jesus, can be interpreted only in the sense of a *servant of God* because even Jesus himself refers to himself as God's servant. This fact is justified by the Verses of the Bible in which many prophets of God, all the way up to Adam, have been termed as the sons of God. Indeed, in Luke, Chapter 3 from verse 22 to verse 38, Jesus is called the son of Joseph, and the genealogy of Joseph is traced to Adam, and Adam is called the son of God. Here is the last portion of these verses:

Luke 3:38

"...which was the son of Enos, which was the son of Seth, which was the son of Adam, which was the son of God."

Seeing this, I thought to myself: *if Jesus is the son of God because he had no father, then Adam should be a greater son of God because not only did he have no father, but no mother either!* To me, this was clear corroboration that the term *son of God* in the bible only means *servant of God*, or *he who has received life from God!* The following questions emerged from my conscience as a result:

Is Jesus the literal Son of God? **No.**

God does not beget and everything already belongs to him anyway.

Is he God incarnate? **No.**

God transcended from such *filth.* He is the omnipotent creator and sustainer of the universe and everything in it; not needy of anything to fulfill his will. In contrast, we clearly see this in the Qur'an:

*"Indeed, His command for something to exist is only to say to it **be** and **it is.**"* – **Qur'an 36:82**

God does not need partners as he is the *almighty*, capable of doing things simply by willing them. I found, during my search for the truth, that this is actually the only point of real difference in the fundamentals between Christianity and Islam; the divinity of Christ.

This created even more complications for me because of the doctrine of the Trinity, which states the following:

- The father is God, the son is God, and the Holy Ghost is God, but they are not 3 gods but 1 God.

- The father is almighty, the son is almighty, and the Holy Ghost is almighty, but they are not 3 almighty(s) but 1 almighty.

- The father is a person, the son is a person, and the Holy Ghost is a person, but they are not 3 persons but 1 person.

Why is it a problem? Well, first of all, the 3 will forever remain 3, i.e., 3 Gods, 3 almighty(s), and 3 persons, simply because of the different *personalities* that this doctrine entails. For example, if you say *In the name of the father,* **and** *the son,* **and** *the Holy Spirit,* you are clearly distinguishing between the 3 of them. As in, when you say *the father,* you are not thinking of the son. And when you say *the son,* you are not thinking of the Holy Ghost. As such, they each have their own intrinsic and individual identity. Therefore, I found that Islam has the strongest claim to Monotheism! If we dissect this further, we find that in all of Christianity it must always be *first* the father, *second* the son, and *third* the Holy Ghost. It would actually be a heresy to start with the son or the Holy Spirit. Hence, if the son is always second in the trinity, how then can they also be one and the same? How can three different things also be one at the same time? How can anything singularly absolute in its unity; containing an indivisible oneness, ever be divided into three separate things with three variant native attributes opposed to each other? And finally, how can its distribution into the three different entities be justifiable? As I thought of these questions, I remained astounded. I also asked myself the following very important question: *which one of these personalities decides when they separate and when they join?* **That** is **the** *God I would worship!* Because of the facts mentioned earlier, the father seems to be that being. Also, does not Jesus himself speak of the father in heaven? We actually see him repeatedly saying the words, *"my father,"* and, *"our father,"* in the bible. If we look at the gospel of Matthew, Jesus says repeatedly: YOUR father, THY father, YOUR father, THY father, a surprising total of 13 TIMES before the first time he finally says MY father! He is telling us that, metaphorically, God is the father of all of us; he does not literally *beget*. This aspect dawned on me like a revelation, but there was even more... all the numerous biblical verses that show others also termed as sons of God. Take a look:

Genesis 6:2
*"the **sons** of God..."*

Exodus 4:22

*"Israel is my **son**, even my first born..."*

Jeremiah 31:9

*"Ephraim is my **son,** even my first born"*

Romans 8:14

*"For as many as are led by the Spirit of God, they are the **sons** of God"*

It was crystal clear to me that the term *son*, or the concept of *sonship* in the bible, obviously means **he who has received life from God**, or **a Godly person**; follow the will of God and you and God will be one in purpose! Finally, I compared all this to the teachings of the Qur'an:

"Allah, there is no deity except Him, The Ever-Living, The Sustainer. Neither drowsiness overtakes Him nor sleep. To Him belongs whatever is in the heavens and whatever is on earth. Who is it that can intercede with Him except by His permission? He knows what is between their hands and what lies behind them, and they encompass not a thing of His knowledge except for what He wills. His throne extends over the heavens and the earth, and their preservation tires Him not, and He is The Exalted, The Great."

– Qur'an 2:255

Islam wants every individual to constantly remember that they will be answerable. It is this jurisprudence that I found beautiful. It wants every human being to have an individual responsibility to virtue against vice, not only in the interest of our own singular life, but also in the interest of the concerted life in this world. Islam continuously invites and encourages toward righteousness, reminding us that we are members of not only the human race, but also of the creation of Allah as a whole. Furthermore, this beautiful religion also continuously warns against wickedness, and reminds us of the consequent punishment from the all-just Lord. Take a look at an example:

> So whoever does a good deed as small as an atom, will see. And whoever does an evil deed as small as an atom, will see.

> **– Qur'an 99:7, 8**

Hence, a true Muslim is kept bound by the concept of responsibility, and remains in constant remembrance of it because of the five daily acts of worship. By knowing that I will meet my lord in worship in just a few hours, this concept revolves around my day and I am constantly reminded that all deeds, no matter how small, are accounted for. Even a simple smile could be counted as a good deed. And Allah is always watching. Always aware.

$$* \sim * \sim * \sim * \sim * \sim * \sim * \sim * \sim *$$

Prophet Mohamad in the Bible

While studying the Bible, I discovered that Prophet Mohamad was actually prophesized in several of its passages. Yes, the All-Merciful Lord has fulfilled his promise: to give mankind the everlasting guidance through his holy prophet until the end of time...

John 14:16

"And I will ask the Father, and he will give you another advocate to help you and be with you forever."

John 16:12 and 13

"I have yet many things to say unto you, but ye cannot bear them now. Howbeit, when he the Spirit of truth is come, he will guide you unto all truth for he shall not speak of himself, but whatsoever he shall hear, that shall he speak; he will show you things to come."

The Acts 3:22 to 25

"For Moses truly said unto the fathers, a prophet shall the Lord your God raise up unto you of your brethren, like unto me, him shall ye hear in all things whatsoever he shall stay unto you. And it shall come to pass, that every soul which will not hear that prophet shall be destroyed from among the people. Yea, and all the prophets from Samuel and

those that follow after, as many as have spoken, have likewise foretold of these days. Ye are the children of the prophets, and of the Covenant which God made with our fathers saying unto Abraham. And in thy seed shall all the kindred of the earth be blessed."

John 16:14

"He shall glorify me: for he shall receive of mine, and shall shew it unto you."

Acts 7:37

"This is that Moses, which said unto the children of Israel, A prophet shall the Lord your God raise up unto you of your brethren, like unto me; him shall ye hear."

A Christian, with a heart full of love for Jesus, might reply saying that these prophecies are about the advent of Jesus himself. In which case I would say: please read these verses again! Does not The Acts 7:37 say that God will raise a prophet *like unto Moses*? Meaning, he will be a man born of a mother *and* a father, as was born Moses, whereas Jesus was born only of a mother. Also, the prophet promised by God must be a man like Moses, but Christians call Jesus the son of God. Furthermore, Moses was a *law giving* prophet, and the one like him must also be a law giver. Jesus, however, was a *law abider*, following the laws of the Ten Commandments previously introduced through Moses. Moreover, one must betray his common sense to say that *I* and *he*, i.e., the first and third person, mean the same. Or that the one who departs prophesizing about the advent of someone else to both be one and the same. Likewise, Jesus said, *"I will pray the Father and he shall give **another** comforter that he may abide with you forever"*. My question is, who is the last known prophet and comforter to man forever? Even if some do not believe in him as a prophet of God, the last prophet known to man after Jesus is still, obviously, none other than Prophet Mohamad to billions of people around the world. Once again, because some of the teachings of Jesus found their way into the Bible, we see glimpses of truth in many of its verses. But what if I told you that Prophet Mohamad was actually even mentioned **by name** in the original Hebrew scripture of the Old Testament? You see, Muslims believe that every prophet has prophesized the advent of the final prophet, Mohamad. And since it is traditionally accepted by many Christians that Prophet Solomon is the author of *The book of Solomon* in the Bible, we see a glimpse of truth emerge from what is otherwise a perverted portrayal of a romantic conversation between (supposedly) Prophet Solomon and his bride; something ill befitting a book revealed from God. Nonetheless, if Prophet Solomon was indeed the author of the originally intended text, before all the obvious fabrications and interpolations, we can see how one of the verses could have been left intact, containing what the prophet actually said. The context here is that Prophet Solomon was preaching to the daughters of Jerusalem, prophesizing about the advent of Prophet Mohamad. He mentions him by name. Take a look at the transliteration of the Hebrew verse:

Hiko mamtakkeem, vekhoullo Mahamad'eem. Zeh dodee veze raee benot yerooshalaim – **The Song of Solomon 5:16**

Translation: *His speech is most sweet; yes, Mohamad. This is my beloved, and this is my friend, O daughters of Jerusalem.*

Prophet Solomon here says, *"His speech is most sweet,"* because Prophet Mohamad is known as the truthful and trustworthy (in Arabic *"Al-Sadequ, Al-ameen");* speaking only truth. Furthermore, Prophet Mohamad is known to have only spoken out of revelation from God. Take a look:

"Your companion [Mohamad] *has not strayed, nor has he erred. Nor does he speak from his own inclination. It is a revelation revealed. Taught by the One acute in strength* [God]*."* – **Qur'an 53:2 – 5**

Knowing that Prophet Mohamad would only speak revelations from God, and being a God loving prophet, it is not surprising to see Prophet Solomon say, *"His speech is most sweet"*.

You might ask, *"Why is there Mahamad'eem as opposed to just plain Mohamad?"* and that would be a very good question. In Hebrew, *eem* is appended to words in order to indicate a plural form. The same concept is used in Arabic, and both languages use these plural forms not only for numbers, but also to extend respect. In the Qur'an, for example, we see God using this plural form to indicate reverence to himself:

> *"It is **We** who give life to the dead and **We** record what they have put forth and what they left behind, and everything **We** have gathered in an apparent leader."* – **Qur'an 36:12**

We clearly see this in the Bible as well. In the book of Genesis, for instance, we see the use of the Hebrew word Elo'**eem**. In Hebrew, Ela means God. Eli also means God. However, Elo'eem means God**s** (plural form). Although translated to English as *God* (singular), the Hebrew term contains the plural of respect, giving reverence to God almighty. This is why Solomon says Mahamad'eem, in plural form; revering Prophet Mohamad. He then says, *"This is my beloved, and this is my friend, O daughters of Jerusalem..."* which is all self-explanatory.

As such, a Muslim embraces every beauty in every religion, and rejects anything that has been added to the religion of God by man, such as the rest of the *Song of Solomon*. I concluded my research with the realization that there can never be another way to please God than to completely surrender ourselves to his will – an act called Islam. I felt fully confident that Islam is an all comprehensive faith, which acknowledges all other religions and contains in it a perfectly complete integration of all the good, found only partly in the other religious orders of the world. The Holy Qur'an is the final exposition of the Divine Truth in its perfection. It was revealed at different times, through the other heavenly scriptures – in parts – suiting the various evolutionary levels of the human intellect. The Qur'an exposes and clarifies all the adulteration and misconceptions that have been fabricated against the original religion of God, some of which are described on the pages that follow. The Qur'an restores the truth.

$$* \sim * \sim * \sim * \sim * \sim * \sim * \sim * \sim *$$

To Desecrate, or Not to Desecrate? That is the Question.

If you make an impartial comparative study of the Old and the New Testaments of the Christian Bible, you will find in them not only many contradictions and discrepancies, but also numeral blasphemies that have been fabricated against Lot, David, Noah, and Abraham; the holy messengers of almighty God. But before I show some of these, let us first take a look at a few contradictions:

Compare this...

"God cannot be tempted with evil, neither tempteth he any man."

– James 1:13

To this...

"And it came to pass after these things, that God did tempt Abraham." **– Genesis 22:1**

Compare this...

"If I bear witness of myself, my witness is not true." **– John 5:31**

To this...

"I am one that bear witness of myself..." **– John 8:18**

Compare this...

"And Jacob called the name of the place Peniel: for I have seen God face to face, and my life is preserved." – **Genesis 32:30**

To this...

"No man hath seen God at any time; the only begotten Son, which is in the bosom of the Father, he hath declared him." – **John 1:18**

And this...

"And I will take away mine hand, and thou shalt see my back parts..." – **Exodus 33:23**

For a comparison with the Qur'an, take a look at what Allah says:

> *"Do they not reflect upon the Qur'an? If it had been from other than Allah, they would have found in it many contradictions."* – **Qur'an 4:82**

As for the blasphemies that have been fabricated against God's holy prophets, take a look:

Genesis 9:20 - 23

"And Noah began [to be] a husbandman, and he planted a vineyard. And he drank of the wine, and was drunken; and

he was uncovered within his tent. And Ham, the father of Canaan, saw the nakedness of his father, and told his two brethren without. And Shem and Japheth took a garment, and laid [it] upon both their shoulders, and went backward, and covered the nakedness of their father; and their faces [were] backward, and they saw not their father's nakedness. "

I could not believe my eyes! I thought: *what emphasizes a message if not the carrier of the message himself?* If any human CEO was to choose someone to deliver a message of good conduct to his employees, he would most certainly choose an employee without flaws in his conduct. Otherwise, what accountability would the message of a CEO have, if he chooses a bad employee to deliver it? Now, is not almighty God, Creator and Sustainer of the multiverse, mighty enough to send infallible messengers to deliver the most important message of all?

Furthermore, also in Genesis, we see Lot committing fornication with his own daughters?! Take a look:

Genesis 19:29

"And it came to pass, when God destroyed the cities of the plain, that God remembered Abraham, and sent Lot out of

the midst of the overthrow, when he overthrew the cities in which Lot dwelt."

Genesis 19:30

"And Lot went up out of Zoar, and dwelt in the mountain, and his two daughters with him; for he feared to dwell in Zoar: and he dwelt in a cave, he and his two daughters."

Genesis 19:31

"And the firstborn said unto the younger, our father [is] old, and [there is] not a man in the earth to come in unto us after the manner of all the earth."

Genesis 19:32

"Come, let us make our father drink wine, and we will lie with him, that we may preserve seed of our father."

Genesis 19:33

"And they made their father drink wine that night: and the firstborn went in, and lay with her father; and he perceived not when she lay down, nor when she arose."

Genesis 19:34

"And it came to pass on the morrow, that the firstborn said unto the younger, Behold, I lay yesternight with my father: let us make him drink wine this night also; and go thou in, [and] lie with him, that we may preserve seed of our father."

Genesis 19:35

"And they made their father drink wine that night also: and the younger arose, and lay with him; and he perceived not when she lay down, nor when she arose."

Genesis 19:36

"Thus were both the daughters of Lot with child by their father."

Genesis 19:37

"And the firstborn bare a son, and called his name Moab: the same [is] the father of the Moabites unto this day."

Genesis 19:38

"And the younger, she also bare a son, and called his name Benammi: the same [is] the father of the children of Ammon unto this day."

Also, in *II Sam. 11* from verse 1 to verse 25, we see David taking possession of his neighbor's wife:

II Samuel 11:4

"And David sent messengers, and took her; and she came in unto him, and he lay with her; for she was purified from her uncleanness: and she returned unto her house."

As I dispassionately read all this, I constantly asked refuge with God from such blasphemies against his holy, infallible, and beloved prophets. I compared, contemplating the fact that Muslims believe in all the prophets of God to be infallible, and that they all possess perfect characters. Consider the following verse from the Qur'an:

"Say [O Mohamad] *we believe in Allah, and that which is revealed unto us, and that which was revealed unto Abraham, and Ishmael, and Isaac, and Jacob, and the tribes, and that which Moses and Jesus received, and that which the prophets received from their lord. We make no distinction between any of them, and unto Him we have surrendered."*

– Qur'an 2:136

The Holy Qur'an further discloses that prophets were raised by God amongst all nations, in all parts of the world:

"...There is not a nation that a warner has not gone among them."

– Qur'an 35:24

And all these prophets are to be taken as role models. Take a look at another Qur'anic verse, which shows the pious reaction of Prophet Joseph when Zulaikha, mentioned in the bible as Potiphar's wife, tries to seduce him:

"And she, in whose house he was, sought to seduce him. She closed the doors and said, 'come to me'. He said 'I seek refuge with Allah. He is my lord who has perfected my reward. Wrongdoers will not succeed.' And she was determined to seduce him and he would have inclined to her, had he not seen the proof of his Lord. And thus it was in order that We avert evil and immorality from him. Indeed, he is of our chosen servants. And they both raced to the door, and she tore his shirt from the back, and they found her husband at the door. She said, 'What is the punishment of a person who intended evil with your wife other than to be imprisoned or a painful torture?' He [Joseph] said, 'It was her who sought to seduce me.' And a witness from her family

testified, 'If his shirt is torn from the front, then she has told the truth, and he is of the liars. But if his shirt is torn from the back, then she has lied, and he is of the truthful.' So when her husband saw his shirt torn from the back, he said 'Indeed, it is a women plan, their plan is great. Joseph, ignore this. And [my wife] ask forgiveness for your sin. Indeed, you made a mistake.'" **– Qur'an 12:23 – 29**

As opposed to what we saw in the bible, these verses of the Holy Qur'an are clearly free of alteration by human hands, redressing the truth to its intended glory. Prophet Jesus knew this, as well as all the prophets that came before. Therefore, they all foretold of the advent of Prophet Mohamad. They had to tell their people to wait until the advent of the *Spirit of Truth* to disclose all the Truth, which is exactly what is seen in John 16 verses 13 and 14. Here they are again for the sake of confirmation:

"Howbeit when he, the Spirit of truth, is come, he will guide you into all truth: for he shall not speak of himself; but whatsoever he shall hear, that shall he speak: and he will show you things to come. He shall glorify me: for he shall receive of mine, and shall shew it unto you."

* ~ * ~ * ~ * ~ * ~ * ~ * ~ * ~ *

Why Not Prophet Mohamad?

Alone in my study, analyzing, correlating, pondering, the following question loomed in my thoughts: *in light of the facts established by such a simple comparative study, why would any Christian not accept Prophet Mohamad as a prophet of God, given that they have accepted all the other thousands of prophets? Why not the seal of them all?* I further reflected: *did not Jesus say that whoever glorifies him is of him? And did not Prophet Mohamad glorify Jesus?*

Indeed, the holy Qur'an not only acknowledges that Jesus is the Messiah from an immaculate conception, but also that he preached the gospel, speaking from as early as the cradle, when he was only two days old. The Qur'an even confirms that Jesus healed the sick, cured the leper, and raised the dead by God's permission. There is even an entire chapter dedicated to his infallible mother, Mariam (*The Virgin Mary*), which is something that even today's bibles do not have. It also gives the good news that Jesus was not crucified, but raised to God alive, and will be back to fight corruption. It is promised by God that Jesus will bring back the earth to its intended glory, alongside a man from the progeny of Prophet Mohamad. The man to whom this book is dedicated.

Some of the facts I just mentioned are seen in the following verses of the holy Qur'an:

"The angels said, 'O Mary, Allah gives you good tidings of a word from Him, whose name will be the Messiah Jesus, son of Mary, distinguished in this world and the hereafter and among those brought near. And he will speak to the people in the cradle and in maturity and will be of the righteous.' She said, 'My Lord, how will I have a child when no man has touched me?' He [The angel] *said, 'Such is Allah; He creates what He wills. When He decrees a matter, He only says to it **be** and it is. And He will teach him the book, wisdom, the Torah, the Gospel, and* [make him] *a messenger to the children of Israel,'* [Jesus will say] *'Indeed I have come to you with a sign from your Lord, in that I create for you from clay* [that which is] *like the form of a bird, and I breathe into it and it becomes a bird by Allah's permission. And I cure the blind and the leper, and I give life to the dead by Allah's permission. And I inform you of what you eat and what you store in your houses. Indeed, in that is a sign for you, if you are believers.'"*

– Qur'an 3:45 – 49

"Rather, Allah raised him [Jesus] *to him. And Allah is Honorable, Wise." –* **Qur'an 4:158**

"The angels said, 'O Mary, indeed Allah has elected, purified, and chosen you from the women of the worlds.'"

– Quran Chapter 3:42

If I had the choice of one thing to say to all my Christian brothers and sisters around the world, I would choose to tell them that Islam is the final annotation of the divine truth; *the last testament.* The comparative analysis we just did shows that Jesus wanted people to know that the spirit of truth, Prophet Mohamad, would guide them into all truth.

* ~ * ~ * ~ * ~ * ~ * ~ * ~ * ~ *

Chapter 8

THE TRUTHFUL

The place suddenly became quiet. They stared at her as if they saw a ghost. The irony is that, if this was a church, my wife could have actually been mistaken for a nun and everything would have been predictably normal. In the restaurant we just entered, however, the crowd seemed suddenly preoccupied by her presence simply because she was wearing her traditional Muslim garments. I remembered how, when we first met, she explained to me that she chose to wear *hijab* not only because it was elected in the Qur'an, but also because it was logic to her. She wanted to be modest. *"I wanted to be completely reserved to my husband,"* she said. She wanted the people she interacted with on a daily basis to focus on her inner beauty, not affected in any way by anything else.

She wanted respect. My thoughts then went further back in time to a particular high school day. I was in the cafeteria with a few classmates. Some were eating their lunch, others were looking over a book, and some were talking and laughing. One girl was wearing *hijab*. She was also talking and having fun, but there was an obvious difference: the guys around the table showed her extra respect. Although they were flirting with some of the girls around the table, the one in the hijab was like a flag: *respect **me**!* I noticed that some girls were actually annoyed by the way the boys were acting with them, but the Muslim girl did not have this problem because they all kept a respectful distance from her. It was in this very moment that I remember thinking to myself: *if I ever have a daughter, that's how I'd want her to be treated.* My attention then sprung back to the current moment, and how my wife and I were being treated. The restaurant was crowded, and most of the patrons were looking at us. The ones not looking seemed to be fighting the urge to look. *"It's ok,"* I told her with a wink. She smiled and said, *"It's unfortunate that some people have successfully tainted our beautiful religion."* As we were welcomed by a waitress and walked in toward our seats, the entire restaurant became even quieter, ostensibly attentive to every step we took.

A man stood up and said,
"Why do you oppress your women by covering them like that, sir? This is a free country!"

I smiled and said,

> *"A true Muslim respects women, especially his wife! If you see a so called Muslim man mistreating his wife, know that these are his personal actions, actually contradicting that which his religion prescribes. In fact, Wearing hijab was her choice, **sir**. And you're right... it **is** a free country!"*

The man, looking at my wife said,

> *"Why do you cover yourself ma'am? Why is Islam so ashamed of women?"*

She replied,

> *"Islam is not ashamed of women. It actually elevates them, treating them as nature treats it jewels... covered and protected from preying eyes."*

Noticing the cross on the man's necklace, I added,

> *"Have you read your bible sir?"*

He said,

> *"Yes I have. I read it every day actually. What's it to you?"*

I continued,

"Have you read 1 Corinthians, chapter 11, verse 6?"

Showing a hint of suspicion, he replied,

"Maybe… Why?"

I said,

"Well sir, it reads 'for if the woman be not covered,
let her also be shorn: but if it be a shame for a
woman to be shorn or shaven, let her be covered.'"

The man was shocked to hear this verse from his own bible; he could not believe it! Opening his smart phone to confirm, he sat down abruptly, looking at his wife across the table and seemingly confused.

I continued,

"Thus, if your wife should be covered according to
*your own bible, why then do you criticize **my** wife for*
her piety, and for following what even the bible
prescribes?"

The man, staring at his phone, shook his head as if admitting defeat. The rest of the restaurant was silently observant of the situation. The waitress put her hand on my wife's shoulder, trying to break the ice with a smile, *"please... have a seat"*.

As we began eating, the man and his wife stood up to leave after finishing their meal. I stood as the man approached our table with his hand extended. It was one of the firmest handshakes anyone had ever given me. *"I love you... brother,"* I said. His wife gave my wife a hug, and they left the restaurant. When I later asked for the bill, to my surprise, I was told that they had paid for our dinner.

As is the case, whenever outside the privacy of one's house, God has commanded every Muslim to have the foresight of wearing attire that avoids impropriety or indecency, as much as is possible, in order to promote and preserve modesty. And this ruling does not apply strictly to women, as many people would have you believe, but also most certainly to men. Just as Muslim women are commanded by God to cover their hair and body with clothing that is loose enough as to prevent body features to be prevalent, Muslim men are also instructed to be dressed such as not to attract; with at least short sleeves as opposed to a tank top as an example, loose clothing as opposed to tight ones as another, and pants covering the entirety of their legs as opposed to shorts as yet another example. As for many Muslim women today, although covering their hair, they nonetheless wear tight and revealing clothing, depicting parts of their bodies that would be inappropriate for me to even mention in my book. Proper hijab is fading away, and many Muslim women are therefore contributing to the portrayal of the false image of Islam. The same is true for many Muslim men, heedless of what is required of them in their attire, let alone their demeanor. Indeed, perfecting one's demeanor inside and outside the house is also part of *hijab*.

Unfortunately, Satan and his followers were able to change the way the beautiful religion of Islam is viewed. Therefore, many things are not as they seem. People accept and believe them simply because they are being told. We have clearly seen in previous chapters that when things are viewed through a typified lens; one that has been tempered with, either by outside forces or even our own inclinations, the blemishes render our understanding blurry or distorted. As such, many people – Muslims and non-Muslims alike – view the Muslim woman as an oppressed person; the victim of a suppressing religion. However, the truth is that hijab is prescribed to women in order for them to be recognized as the peak of purity and virtue; the peak of eloquence even before beginning to speak – a flag for piety and devotion. Yes, *Hijab* is a flag! If my daughter has to be somewhere alone with a man, I would hope this man is a devout Muslim who understands *hijab* and, therefore, lowers his gaze in respect to her purity and virtue. He would speak to her while keeping a respectful distance, knowing that God is always watching.

Allah says in the Qur'an:

> *"O prophet, tell your wives and your daughters and the women of the believers to bring down upon themselves from their garments.* ***This is so that they become known,*** *and not be hurt. And Allah is Forgiving and Merciful."*

– Qur'an 33:59

Unfortunately, in many societies, women are not only encouraged to show more skin, but are also influenced to conform to the belief that they are still in control; a perfect example of the prison with invisible walls mentioned in chapter 3, *The Twilight of Falsehood*. This is the psychological elaborateness of mind-manipulation, which transposes the victim to a state in which the feeling of acting on one's own initiative is ever present. Nonetheless, women in these societies are *"free"* in every sense of the word, and the astute will once more read between the lines. A women in hijab, however, is the exemplar of ability and freedom, having freed herself from the shackles of society... *to preserve her value.*

* ~ * ~ * ~ * ~ * ~ * ~ * ~ * ~ *

The Word *Islamophobia* Makes No Sense!

Although terrorists call themselves Muslims, the truth is that they
cannot be. The religion of Islam actually condemns acts of evil and
terror, and promotes not only the preservation of life – human or
other – but also its protection and nourishment, regardless of which
religion, race, color, ethnicity, or any other background a person
might be from. True Islam; not the one you see on television,
actually forbids to hurt even a fly... ***literally***. Islam promotes love,
tolerance, sharing, and caring. It merely presents its facts for the
sake of providing its good news, without forcing anyone into
embracing it. The evil deeds you see done by *so called Muslims* have
nothing to do with the religion, and are from that evil person's own
accord. This concept is clarified in many passages of the Holy
Qur'an, such as in chapter 109:

> *In the name of Allah The Compassionate, The Merciful*
> *Verse 1 – Say* [O Mohamad], *O you who disbelieve.*
> *Verse 2 – I do not worship what you worship.*
> *Verse 3 – Nor are you worshipping what I worship.*
> *Verse 4 – Nor am I worshipping what you worshipped.*
> *Verse 5 – Nor are you worshipping what I worship.*
> *Verse 6 – **You have your religion, and I have one**.*

In other words, the religion of Islam is clear: *any person is free to worship whatever they want.*

This is also seen in chapter 2:

> *Verse 256 -* **There is no compulsion in religion.** *Right from wrong has been revealed...*

And chapter 36:

> *Verse 17 - And the messenger's responsibility is* **only** *to give clear notification.*

Hence, Islam only presents its facts, warning us of a day of judgement on which we will be adjudicated based on our deeds, and explains the intricacies of existence, the universe, as well as our purpose in the grand scheme of things. Islam establishes a peaceful and serene way of life. It presents the teachings of one hundred and twenty four thousand prophets including Adam, Noah, Jonas, Joseph, Abraham, Moses, Jesus, and Mohamad. One has to see the truth for himself and fully understand, either accepting or rejecting it. Islam promotes freedom of choice and allows people to live their lives as they wish, as long as they are not hurting others.

However, since the dawn of time, there has always been a battle between good and evil. Ever since Adam and Eve were created, Satan has been whispering in the hearts of mankind, and his focus has always been God's prophets. Satan and his minions have always worked on corrupting the message that God's messengers came forth with. Prophet Mohamad is the most important prophet of all, bringing the religion that started with Adam to its intended completion, and Satan knows this very well. Therefore, he went to work. Now, many people ignorantly criticize Prophet Mohamad, contending, for example, that *he spread the religion of Islam by waging wars*. These people attack the prophet without even taking the time to confirm these fallacies. Unfortunately, they believe what they hear, see, or read, without any cross reference to certify the validity of the information they receive. As seen earlier, even many Muslims today portray to non-Muslims the wrong image of Islam. People see them and think, *"So this is Islam? This is what Mohamad taught?"* All this is due to human beings' limited perspective, thinking that what they see or hear is all there is; the truth. I say to these people: Learn about Prophet Mohamad from the correct sources; the sources that do not have the fingerprint of Satan all over them.

Greek philosopher *Plato* has a beautiful analogy about the subject of limited perspective in his work, *The Republic*, also narrated by Greek philosopher *Socrates*. The analogy states that human beings are like people chained to a wall inside a cave. They are chained by their feet and necks, and they cannot move. The only thing these people see is another wall in front of them. There are shadows on the wall. The prisoners believe that the shadows are all that exists in the world they inhabit. They even start to give names to the shadows. The analogy explains that if one of these prisoners is freed from the chains, and walked to peek behind the wall he was chained on, he would see a fire and some *other* people casting the shadows like puppeteers. Furthermore, if the freed person would walk to the exit of the cave, he would be able to lay his eyes upon the beauty of the world outside.

As such, many people – *stuck in a cave* – ignorantly ascribe evil attributes to Islam and its prophet, heedless of *the other people casting the shadows*. Heedless of *the world outside*. Heedless of the truth. The irony is that none of the fabrications made against Prophet Mohamad even fit his character and/or personality! And what people sometimes forget is that Prophet Mohamad was sent by God at a time of extremely harsh circumstances. The Arabian Peninsula was a barren and desolate region with scorching sun and oppressive heat by day, and chilling cold by night. For the people that lived there, morality was dictated merely by necessity, and many lived as savage beasts who even buried their newborn daughters alive because it was not a boy. The prophet began receiving revelations from God in Mecca during 610 CE. He was appointed to carry, preach, and protect the sacred message, presenting the *last testament* to mankind until the day of judgement. He started by criticizing the Meccans, especially the family and companions of a man by the name of *Abu Sufian*, for worshipping idols and mistreating the weak. The prophet followed by purchasing slaves in order to free them. Therefore, with their lifestyle threatened by the caring Prophet Mohamad, and seeing that he is working on eradicating racism, slavery, and oppression, the Meccans became hostile, tortured many Muslims, and even went as far as to kill many others. Some of the remaining Muslims escaped to Abyssinia, a Christian city southwest of Mecca. The Meccans followed them and tried to convince the Abyssinian emperor to turn them over...

The emperor of Abyssinia walked into the throne room where the Muslims were waiting, followed by a few Meccan men that had pursued the Muslims hoping to convince the emperor to turn them over. Many Abyssinians were also standing in the room, along with 300 Meccan guards, awaiting the verdict of their emperor. When he reached his throne, everybody bowed in reverence except the Muslims. Noticing this, one of the Meccans whispered to his friend,

"Good! Their stiff neck will hang them."

When everybody raised, the emperor said,

"Do you not bow yourselves before your prophet?"

One of the Muslims, Jafar, Imam Ali's brother, replied,

"Mohamad is a man. We kneel only to God."

The Meccan said,

"Where are Mohamad's miracles, Jafar? If he were a prophet, he'd light the sky with miracles."

The emperor continued,

"Indeed this is true. God has given his prophets a sign of miracles, that we may recognize them."

Jafar promptly replied,

"One of Mohamad's miracles is the Holy Qur'an."

The Meccan said mockingly,

"A book!? A book?! I think the emperor's had enough..."

The emperor continued,

"When God sent tongues of fire upon the heads of Christ's apostles, so they could speak the many languages of the world that they knew not before... but do such miracles happen in our times? I've heard enough! You've made a poor case! Lock them up."

As the emperor's wardens approached the Muslims with chains, Jafar yelled,

> *"When we suffered persecution in Mecca, Mohamad told us to go to Abyssinia, the land of a righteous king where no man is wronged."*

The Meccan interrupted him saying,

> *"What they call persecution was fair punishment, because of the disorder they caused..."*

The emperor interrupted him,

> *"Why did your prophet send you to me?"*

Jafar replied,

> *"Because you believe in the book of the one God as we do, he sent us because, in your heart, God will protect us."*

The Meccan,

> *"Talking to them is like drawing water from a mirage!"*

The emperor replied,

> *"But they've now laid a duty on me to listen to them, my friend."*

He ordered his people to remove the chains,

"*Go on...*" the emperor said attentively.

Jafar took a few steps toward the emperor,

"*For years, we worshiped wood and stone; images of our own manufacture. We lived in ignorance of God. We had few earthly laws and no heavenly laws. The rich neglect the poor, and the natural pity of man, whereby he lifts his brother up when he has fallen, is despised by them* (pointing at the Meccans) *as 'upsetting social order'. To this inhumanity has come a man whom God chose, and in that we believe.*"

The emperor,

"*You are overcome... I beg you to collect yourself.*"

Jafar, calming down,

"*I speak of the messenger of God. Mohamad teaches us to worship one God, to speak truth, to love our neighbors as ourselves, to give charity, even a smile can be charity, to protect women from misuse, to shelter orphans, and to turn away from Gods of wood and stone!*"

The Meccan angrily said,

> *"I cannot keep still and hear this blasphemy! We are an ancient civilization... to call our gods wood and stone is to speak ignorantly of them. The idol... the form is not what we worship, but the spirit that resides within the form."*

The emperor added,

> *"I agree that idolatry isn't always fully understood."*

The Meccan,

> *"Thank you! Now let me bring him back to the women..."*

Jafar promptly said,

> *"God made women to be the proper companions of men. They are different, but equal..."*

The Meccan interrupted him mockingly saying,

> *"Equal?! We buy them, feed them, clothe them, use them, and discard them. Women... equal to us?!"*

While the Meccans were laughing aloud, Jafar continued,

> *"God created man from one male and one female.*
> (Turning towards the Meccans) *You must respect in
> all women the womb that bore you?"*

Silence reigned for a few moments…

The emperor then said to the Meccans,

> *"Why are your 300 guards so tongue tied?"*

Jafar continued,

> *"God has spoken to us before through Abraham,
> Noah, Moses, and through Jesus. Why should we be
> so surprised that God speaks to us now through
> Mohamad?"*

The emperor abruptly replied,

> *"Who taught you those names?"*

Jafar said,

> *"They are names in the Qur'an."*

The Meccan,

> *"We knew Mohamad when he was an orphan
> minding sheep…"*

The emperor replied,

> *"And we knew Christ as a carpenter... what Christ says, and what your Mohamad says, is like two raised from the same lap."*

The Meccan,

> *"They are lying to you. They deny Christ... you worship three Gods they say, father, son, and Holy Ghost they say."*

The emperor asked the Muslims,

> *"What do you say of Christ?"*

The Meccan interrupted,

> *"They say God cannot have a son! Christ is not the son of God!"*

The emperor asked them again,

> *"Speak to me of Christ!"*

Jafar said,

> *"We say of Christ what our prophet has taught us. That God cast his spirit into the womb of a virgin named Mary, and that she conceived Christ, the apostle of God."*

The Meccan again interrupted,

"The apostle he says! Not the son... not the son!!"

The emperor stood up and walked toward the Muslims,

"What does your miracle, the Qur'an, say about our dear lord Jesus Christ?"

Jafar asked if he may relay the words. The emperor took a few steps forward, asking Jafar to come closer to him. Jafar came and recited a few verses of *surah Mariam*,

"In the name of God, The Compassionate, The Merciful. Relay in the book the story of Mary. How she withdrew from her family to a place in the east. So she veiled herself from them. So We sent to her our spirit [the angel Gabriel], *and he presented himself to her in human form. She said, 'I seek refuge from you in The Merciful, if you fear God. He said, 'I am a messenger from your Lord to announce the birth of a pure son to you'. She said, 'how shall I have a son when no man has touched me, and have not been unchaste?' He* [Gabriel] *replied, 'This is what your Lord said; it is easy for me. And We will make him a sign for people, and a mercy from us. It is a matter decreed'."* **– Qur'an 19:16 – 21**

The emperor took a few more steps closer to Jafar and said,

"The difference between us and you…"

Drawing a line on the ground between him and Jafar, he continued,

"…is no thicker than this line."

He turned toward the Meccans and said,

"Not for a mountain of gold would I give them up to you! O Muslims, you may live in Abyssinia in peace for as long as you wish, and may God's blessings be upon you on your return."

* ~ * ~ * ~ * ~ * ~ * ~ * ~ * ~ *

Twelve years later...

In 622 CE, after an attempt by the Meccans to assassinate him, Prophet Mohamad and his followers retreated to a nearby city called Medina, at the invitation of a group of people who had become Muslim. Because the prophet and his followers left everything behind to suddenly migrate to Medina, the Meccans seized the opportunity to confiscate their homes and belongings. The prophet left Mecca so he could live in peace and build a new society in the more welcoming city of Medina. From there, as a messenger of almighty God, he continued to criticize the Meccans for worshipping idols and mistreating the weak. He had to defend! The Meccans demanded that the people of Medina expel the prophet and turn him over. They even threatened to attack Medina if the prophet was not brought to them. Small groups of Meccans traveled to the outskirts of Medina, got into skirmishes with Muslim troops, and seized livestock from Medina – a very oppressive ordeal! Therefore, Muslims from Medina seized Meccan trading caravans passing near their city. These caravans were owned by the wealthy Meccans who abused people and spread corruption. Many people use these arguments to say that Prophet Mohamad spread the religion of Islam by waging wars. However, any sensible person will affirm that the seizure of Meccan caravans was not an offensive act by the Muslims, but a defensive one. Did Muslims seize the Meccan caravans simply because they were non-Muslim caravans? Of course not! The Muslims seized these caravans in retaliation for the

Meccan's coup back in Mecca, as well as in response to the Meccan seizure of Muslim property, which left many Muslims without financial resources. Furthermore, the Muslims seized the Meccan caravans because they knew that the revenue generated by them would be used to finance Mecca's threatened attacks on Medina. Would you not have done the same to protect the people? Any rational person would. Contrary to what many ignorant people would have you believe, Prophet Mohamad was not a war monger, but was responsibly protecting the weak by fighting the corrupt in self-defense, as well as using preemptive measures to prevent potential future threats.

In 624 CE, the second year after the prophet moved to Medina, a Meccan army marched towards Medina to fight the Muslims. In response, a Muslim army marched from Medina and fought the Meccans at *Badr*, an area close to Medina, and the Muslims won the battle. In view of this, was the march of a Muslim army to Badr an act of attack or defense? Again, as a messenger of God with a promise to fulfill and protect a sacred message, Prophet Mohamad **had** to defend. Would you not? Any prudent person would! Especially when the enemy's goal was to destroy Islam. A year after the battle of Badr, in 625 CE, yet another Meccan army marched toward Medina to fight the Muslims. In response, a Muslim army met the Meccan army near *Mount Uhud*, a mountain north of Medina. The Meccans won the battle because many of the Muslims did not follow Prophet Mohamad's orders, allowing the Meccans to flank and scatter them.

Following the battle of Uhud, the Muslims expelled one of the Jewish tribes from Medina, named *Banu Nadir*, after having attempted to assassinate the prophet. The tribe moved north to the Jewish city of *Khaybar*, while other Jewish tribes remained peacefully in Medina. In 627 CE, two years after the battle of Uhud, an army of Meccans and their allies from northern Arabia – Arabs and Jews who had been expelled from Medina, as well as Jews from Khaybar – marched toward Medina for battle. The Muslims dug a massive trench around Medina in order to prevent the enemy's cavalry units from crossing, and to also render their horsemen vulnerable if they entered the trench. This battle became known as *the battle of the trench*. Unable to cross and attack the Muslims, the Meccans and their allies surrounded and besieged Medina for a month. One of the enemy's men by the name of *Amr, son of Abdul-Wod*, known for his strength and brutality, was able to have his horse jump over the trench and reach the Muslim side of the battle, taunting them. Prophet Mohamad asked his men, *"Who is for Amr?"* As in, *who is ready to fight him?* Everyone stayed quietly in fear, except Imam Ali, son of Abi Taleb, who stood and said, *"I am, O messenger of Allah!"* And when the brave Ali – only in his twenties at the time – rode confidently toward the dangerous Amr, the prophet said, *"All of faith has stood to confront all of idolatry"*. Amr mocked the Muslims for sending a young boy to fight the experienced great warrior he was. When the dust settled… Amr was lying dead on the ground. Eventually, the Meccans and their allies ended the siege and returned to their homes. Many anti-Muslims criticize Prophet Mohamad for having killed many men from a Jewish tribe after the battle of the trench. But none of these anti-Muslims give the reason for the executions, withholding the information in order to make the prophet look evil. Yes, Prophet Mohamad did execute many men from a Jewish tribe called *Banu Qurayza*. But why? Well… for treason. You see, prior to the Battle, the Banu Qurayza were living peacefully in Medina and had entered into a mutual defense treaty with the Muslims. However, they were relentless in aiding the Meccans and their allies in their attempt to defeat the Muslims and kill the prophet during the Battle of the trench. Hence, when one knows the reason, astonishment dissipates. Therefore, Prophet Mohamad did not *"just fight wars,"* as some might say. He did not *"spread the religion by the sword"* like others say. In light of these facts, it should be obvious that Satan's plan is to destroy God's image. As a result, Prophet Mohamad was not only attacked back then, but the onslaught never stopped… even today, only because he was involved in several wars. But this is no surprise now, is it? In fact, if the prophet was not a master at war, i.e., a *war general*, we would not have Islam today! Is it actually not a noble deed to fight evil in defense of good?

If your enemy attacks your home, would you not become a noble *war general* and defend your family? What if you were also tasked with protecting the people and the most sacred message of all? I remain shocked that some people find it surprising that Prophet Mohamad was involved in wars, due to the harsh circumstances of his time. Thus, although Islam promotes peace, it is not a pacifistic religion. And if the correct history is read, it becomes clear that *turning the other cheek* would have resulted in success for the corrupt... something that Prophet Mohamad did all he could to prevent. Allow me to present a helpful analogy:

> *"But I say unto you, that ye resist not evil: but whosoever shall smite thee on thy right cheek, turn to him the other also"* – **Matthew 5:39**

Although the United States of America believes Jesus to have said the above mentioned words, and the U.S. dollar bill contains the words, *"In God we trust,"* it still employs armed forces to defend against evil – sometimes even using preemptive measures. And I tell you that, as a citizen of this country, I would be proud to bear arms against evil and corruption in defense of the U.S.A. and its people. And this is exactly what Prophet Mohamad did... he protected.

It is a worldwide fact that Prophet Mohamad is – and will always be – the most influential single figure in human history. Why is that? Because he was a crook? Would that even make sense? Because he was *a tyrant who only fought wars*? Do you think that all the Muslims in the world today would accept to be influenced by such a leader? If anybody says yes, I tell them: have you looked at the number of Muslims in the world today? According to Time magazine, by 2030, the global population is set to reach over 8 billion humans, and 26.4% of that population will be Muslim. Furthermore, a report by the Pew Forum on Religion and Public Life titled *The Future of the Global Muslim Population* projects that the number of Muslims in the world is set to double from 1.1 billion in 1990, to 2.2 billion in 2030. If you think that all these people are *blind Muslims* influenced by a tyrant, you are free to do so, but you cannot expect many others to betray their common sense. I tell you: the reason there are so many Muslims in the world today, and that Islam is the fastest growing religion on earth, is because Prophet Mohamad is the trustworthy, the gentleman, the concerned, the kind, and the brave. He freed slaves, adopted orphans, and promoted good and condemned evil. He is the generous, *the truthful*, the last prophet of God, the *seal* of the prophets, and God's most beloved creation. He is… **Mohamad!**

The English definition of the name Mohamad is ***The praised one***.
And he is undeniably worthy of praise.

A great non-Muslim man who obviously read the correct history once said:

"I became more than convinced that it was not the sword that won a place for Islam in those days in the scheme of life. It was the rigid simplicity, the utter self-effacement of the prophet, his scrupulous regard for pledges, his intense devotion to his friends and followers, his intrepidity, his fearlessness, his absolute trust in God and in his own mission." – **Mahatma Gandhi, 1924**

Chapter 9

REVERBERATING ECHO

Merciful and caring, Prophet Mohamad is known to have had the most radiant smile. He was a role model. Yet after his death, many continued their oppression by further ascribing false traditions *(hadiths)* to him... even today. For one, contrary to popular belief, there is no mention of *stoning* anywhere in the Qur'an. The irony is that stoning is instead mentioned in many passages of the bible. Hard to believe? Take a look:

> *"If there be found among you, within any of thy gates which the Lord thy God giveth thee, man or woman, that hath wrought wickedness in the sight of the Lord thy God, in transgressing his covenant, And hath gone and served other gods, and worshipped them, either the sun, or moon, or any*

of the host of heaven, which I have not commanded; And it be told thee, and thou hast heard of it, and enquired diligently, and, behold, it be true, and the thing certain, that such abomination is wrought in Israel: Then shalt thou bring forth that man or that woman, which have committed that wicked thing, unto thy gates, even that man or that woman, and shalt stone them with stones, till they die."

– Deuteronomy 17:2, 3, 4, 5

"If a man have a stubborn and rebellious son, which will not obey the voice of his father, or the voice of his mother, and that, when they have chastened him, will not hearken unto them: Then shall his father and his mother lay hold on him, and bring him out unto the elders of his city, and unto the gate of his place; And they shall say unto the elders of his city, This our son is stubborn and rebellious, he will not obey our voice; he is a glutton, and a drunkard. And all the men of his city shall stone him with stones, that he die: so shalt thou put evil away from among you; and all Israel shall hear, and fear." **– Deuteronomy 21:18, 19, 20, 21**

"And he that blasphemeth the name of the LORD, he shall surely be put to death, and all the congregation shall certainly stone him: as well the stranger, as he that is born

in the land, when he blasphemeth the name of the LORD,
shall be put to death." – **Leviticus 24:16**

"A man also or woman that hath a familiar spirit, or that is
a wizard, shall surely be put to death: they shall stone them
with stones: their blood shall be upon them."

– **Leviticus 20:27**

In the Qur'an, also contrary to popular belief, there is no mention of *seventy two virgins in heaven* either. Furthermore, there is no such thing as *sharia law*, which is actually a flawed fabrication because both words mean the same thing, i.e., the Arabic word *sharia* actually also means *law*. You see, every religion has its law and jurisprudence to dictate what is right from wrong, and that is simply what the Arabic word *sharia* means. Therefore, if we translate the fabrication of *"sharia law,"* it becomes *"law law"* and does not make any sense!? Moreover, Prophet Mohamad did not *marry a nine year old*. You see, historians have established that the prophet's wife, *Aisha*, was ten years younger than her sister *Asmaa*, who was born seventeen years before the prophethood of Prophet Mohamad. The preaching of the prophet was known to have lasted thirteen years in Mecca before his migration to Medina. Thirteen years in Mecca, plus seventeen years before, means that Asmaa was no less than thirty years old at the time of the prophet's migration to

Medina. And if Aisha was ten years younger than her sister, then she was twenty years old when the prophet migrated. And finally, since they married during the second year after the migration, Aisha was twenty two years old. The people who attack the prophet by saying that *he married a nine year old girl* are only thirteen years off!? Not bad... let us swiftly move on. Also contrary to what even many Muslims believe, and this might surprise a lot of people, Prophet Mohamad was **NOT** illiterate. This was falsely attributed to him due to a discrepancy in the translation of the Arabic word *ommey*. You see, the word *ommey* has many meanings, one of which is indeed *cannot read or write*. However, the Qur'anic verse which speaks of Prophet Mohamad's origin uses the word *ommey* to mean *from mecca*. Mecca was known as *the mother of villages*, and the word *ommey* also means *related to the mother*.

Therefore, the Qur'anic verse in question with the **incorrect** interpretation is as follows:

> It is He who has sent among the ***unlettered*** a Messenger from themselves reciting to them his verses, and purifying them, and teaching them the Book and wisdom. Although they were before in clear error – **Qur'an 62:2 (incorrect)**

On the other hand, take a look at the **correct** interpretation:

> *"It is He who has sent in the people, from **the mother of villages** [**Mecca**], a Messenger from themselves to recite to them his verses, and purify them, and teach them the Book and wisdom. Even if they were apparently deviating before."*
>
> **– Qur'an 62:2**

And to confirm that what is meant by the word *ommey* is not *illiterate*, but rather *from the mother of villages*, also take a look at another verse which clearly shows the same word. This time, however, usually translated correctly:

> *"And thus We have revealed to you an Arabic Qur'an in order to warn **the mother of villages** [**Mecca**], and those around it..."* **– Qur'an 42:7**

Furthermore, how could the prophet *"...recite to them his verses, and purify them, and teach them the Book and wisdom..."* if he is *illiterate*? It would not make any sense. However, even in light of these facts, many people still hold on to the idea, and I know the reason why. They think that having been able to offer so much scientific explanations on the intricacies of the multiverse while having been *illiterate* creates further proof of his prophethood. I tell you: there is no need for this. Prophet Mohamad's prophethood has been proven with countless unequivocal facts, such as the ones provided in this book... if only we reflect.

The problem that arises due to mistranslations causes the misunderstanding of even subtle aspects of the religion of Islam. For example, Muslims do not pray **only** five times a day. Surprised? I do not blame you. You see, the five daily *prayers* that Muslims perform are, more accurately, *acts of worship*; not strictly prayers. Even many Arabic speaking Muslims today do not know this because the word *prayer* has become well established; *"Its prayer time son, get ready,"* or, *"Did you guys pray yet? Why not? What time is prayer today?"* In actuality, the Arabic term used for the five daily rituals is *salaat (worship)*. Prayer, on the other hand, is a subtly different concept pronounced *doaa'*, which ultimately means *supplication*. Although the five daily acts of worship do contain supplications *(doaa')*, they are decisively a constructive act of adoration, devotion, and worship. As such, Muslims do not pray **only** five times a day, but actually have countless amounts of fascinating *prayers* for every day of the week, and for different times during each day throughout the entire year. Take, for example, the mesmerizing words of the *morning's supplication*, which we read very early in the day after the morning *worship*...

The Morning's Supplication

By Imam Ali, son of Abi Taleb

In the Name of God, the Compassionate, the Merciful

O God, O He who extended the morning's tongue in the speech of its dawning, and dispatched the fragments of the dark night into the gloom of its stammering, and mastered the creation of the turning spheres in the measures of its display, and beamed forth the brightness of the sun in the light of its blazing. O He who guided toward himself with himself, and transcended from congeniality with His creatures, and is exalted beyond conformity with His methods.

O He who is near to the passing thoughts, far from the regards of eyes, and knows what will be before it comes to be. O He who has put me at ease in the cradle of His security and sanctuary, awakened me to the favors and kindness that He has bestowed upon me, and held me from the claws of evil with His hand and His power.

Bless, O God, the guide to Thee [Prophet Mohamad] *in the darkest night. He who, of Thy reasons, clings to the cord of the tallest honor. Him whose glory is evident at the summit of stout shoulders, and whose feet were entrenched in spite of slippery places in the previous era, and bless his household, the good, the chosen, the pious. And open for us, O God, the doors of the morning with the keys of mercy and prosperity. Clothe me, O God, with the most excellent robes of guidance and righteousness. Plant, O God, through Thy tremendousness, the springs of humility in the watering place of my heart. Cause to flow, O God, because of Thy reverence, tears from the corner of my eyes, and chastise, O God, the recklessness of my clumsiness with the reins of contentment.*

My God, if mercy from Thee does not begin with fair success for me, then who can take me to Thee upon the evident path? If Thy deliberateness would turn me over to the guide of hope and wishes, then who will annul my slips from the stumbles of caprice? If Thy help should forsake me in the battle with the soul and Satan, then Thy forsaking will have entrusted me to where there is hardship and deprivation. My God, dost Thou see that I have only come to Thee from the direction of hopes, or clung to the ends of Thy cords when my sins have driven me from the house of union?

So what an evil mount upon which my soul has mounted - its caprice! Woe upon it for being seduced by its own opinions and wishes! And destruction be upon it for its audacity toward its Master and Protector! My God, I have knocked upon the door of Thy mercy with the hand of my hope, fled to Thee seeking refuge from my excessive caprice, and fixed the fingers of my love to the ends of Thy cords.

So pardon, O God, the slips and errors I have committed, and release me from the foot tangling of my robe. For Thou art my Master, my Protector, my Support, and my Hope. And Thou art the object of my search and my desire in my ultimate end and stable abode. My God, how couldst Thou drive away a poor beggar who seeks refuge in Thee from sins, fleeing? Or how couldst Thou disappoint one seeking guidance who headed to Thy threshold, striving? Or how couldst thou deny one that is thirsty who arrived to your ponds, drinking?

Never! For Thy pools are full in the hardship of drought, Thy door is open for seeking and penetration, and Thou art the goal of requests and the object of hopes. My God, these are the reins of my soul, I have bound them with the ties of Thy will. These are the burdens of my sins, I have averted them with Thy pardon and mercy. And these are my caprices that lead astray, I have entrusted them to the threshold of Thy gentleness and kindliness.

So make this morning of mine, O God, descend upon me with the radiance of guidance, and with safety in religion and the world! And make my evening a shield against the deception of enemies, and a protection against the destructive blows of caprice.

Verily, Thou art able over what Thou wilt! Thou givest the kingdom to whom Thou wilt, and Thou seizest the kingdom from whom Thou wilt; Thou exaltest whom Thou wilt, and Thou abasest whom Thou wilt; in Thy hand is the good; Thou art powerful over all things. Thou makest the night to enter into the day, and Thou makest the day to enter into the night; Thou bringest forth the living from the dead, and Thou bringest forth the dead from the living; and Thou providest whomsoever Thou wilt without reckoning. There is no God but Thou! Glory be to Thee, O God, and Thine is the praise! Who knows Thy measure without fearing Thee? Who knows what Thou art without awe of Thee? Through Thy power, Thou hast joined disparate things, through Thy gentleness Thou hast cleaved apart the daybreak. And through Thy generosity, Thou hast illumined the dark shrouds of night. Thou hast made waters, sweet and salt, flow forth from hard shining stones, sent down out of rain-clouds water cascading, and appointed the sun and the moon as a blazing lamp for creatures, without experiencing in that which Thou originated either weariness or effort.

So, O He who is alone in might and subsistence, and dominates His servants with death and annihilation, Bless Mohamad and his household, the righteous. Hear my call, destroy my enemies, answer my supplication, and actualize through Thy bounty my hope and desire.

O best of those who is called to remove affliction, and is the object of hope in every difficulty and ease. I have stated my need from you, so do not reject me, O my master, despairing of Thy exalted gifts. O All-generous! O All-generous! O All-generous! By Thy mercy, O Most Merciful of the merciful. Bless the best of your creations, Mohamad and his household. Amen.

My God, my heart is veiled, my soul deficient, my mind defeated, my caprice triumphant, my obedience little, my disobedience much, and my tongue acknowledges sin. So what am I to do? O He who knows the unseen things! O He who forgives sins! O He who covers defects! Forgive all my sins! O Forgiver! O Forgiver! O Forgiver! O He who has rigid punishment! O Pardoner, O Merciful! O Clement, O Generous! Fulfill my needs in the greatness of the Qur'an, and the generous prophet! And bless Mohamad and the household of Mohamad, the good, the pure. Amen.

* ~ * ~ * ~ * ~ * ~ * ~ * ~ * ~ *

Prayer is powerful enough to open doors and change destiny. The day's door is locked, and the above morning supplication is the key. In fact, all of life's locked doors have a master key: prayer. We might not see, smell, feel, hear, nor taste with a direct apparatus, but prayer flows through the process of transduction uncontaminated by falsehood and – eventually – directly loosens the knots of inevitability by shaping our synapses. Islam teaches us that through constant prayer we acquire safeguard, dissolve adversity, secure blessing, allow supplication, lengthen hope, avoid tribulation, and shape our destiny. As we have seen earlier, that which our senses perceive is not definitive, and reality must be sought from the personal sanctum that exists within the core of our being. But the Sanctum is locked. The key? Prayer...

* ~ * ~ * ~ * ~ * ~ * ~ * ~ * ~ *

Everything Happens for a Reason

Sayed Mohamad Mehdi Baher Al-Oloom, son of *Sayed Mortada*, son of *Mohamad Brujerde Tabataba'ee Baher Al-Oloom*, was a great and famous Muslim scholar of the twelfth century. He died at the age of fifty seven, and was buried next to the grave of *Sheikh Al-Tusi* in the shrine of Imam Ali, son of Abi Taleb. Sayed Baher Al-Oloom came from an excellent, very righteous and pious family. His father, Sayed Mortada, was himself a very well-known scholar. In a dream, Sayed Mortada saw Imam Ali Al-Reda giving him a brightly-lit candle, which was supposed to represent the light of knowledge and guidance his son would bring to the world. One day, when Sayed Baher Al-Oloom was very young, he saw a man carrying water passing by. As the man approached, he used a sharp tool to make a tear in the waterskin. The water spilled, and the man turned to Sayed Mortada, complaining about his son's action. Sayed Mortada apologized to him, asking him what it would cost to replace his loss. The man received compensation and left. Baher Al-Oloom's mother was surprised by her son's act and, because she understands that everything happens for a reason, she asks her husband for his opinion as to why he thinks their son did this. He reminds her of a time when she was pregnant with Baher Al-Oloom and they were in an orchard. *"Remember?"* He tells her... *"You saw a tree with a beautiful apple on it that attracted you."* Indeed, while pregnant, anything the mother does affects the baby she is carrying. Hence, mothers have an immense responsibility during pregnancy. Islam emphasizes this in its teachings, showing that women are the streams of education and nourishment for all generations that follow. They are carrying a spirit within their spirit and, therefore, have a responsibility to not only stay away from that which might affect the baby negatively, but to also perform certain deeds that will have a positive effect on the child. As for Baher Al-Oloom's mother, the orchard they were in did not belong to them. *"You saw the apple..."* her husband tells her, *"...and you were attracted by how delicious it looked, but you felt it would be wrong to take. First, because the place did not belong to us; you did not have permission. Second, because you weren't hungry and, accordingly, you would be satisfying a want, not a need. And third, because you thought of the fact that you were pregnant."* This is how a true God fearing Muslim thinks. We have to take all the angles of any situation into consideration, no matter how small the effect might be, and confirm that no harm to anything in this world would come from our actions. Imagine how life on our lovely planet would be if all human beings took all the angles of any situation into consideration in this same way. He tells her, *"Back then, when you realized all this, you took one of the pins holding your scarf and, without plucking it from the tree, you poked the apple with your pin and tasted it."* This is actually an amazing realization which shows the extent to which we have to be careful of any action we take. *"That pin…"* he tells her, *"…turned into a little pocket knife today."* When we understand this, we realize that most of the events in our lives are there because we attract them there. If we change our thinking system, and constantly request from God in prayer to make us better beings, the events of our lives will change as a result.

$$* \sim * \sim * \sim * \sim * \sim * \sim * \sim * \sim *$$

The teachings of Prophet Mohamad make the world a better place, and he himself says: *"I have come to perfect moral character"*. Thus, the religion of Islam, if followed as prescribed by Allah, makes the world a better place for all. However, after the death of the prophet, people – many of which actually call themselves Muslims – have been plotting to destroy the message he brought forth, and what better way than to ascribe evil attributes to the religion and its prophet? As we have seen, there is no such thing as *moderate Muslims*, nor is there such a thing as *radical Islam*, and *Islamophobia* is nonsense. These are all interpolations made to fool people into believing that the religion of Islam is evil, and that, however, some of its followers are *moderate* about it. The truth is, you are either a Muslim or you are not. And the truth always prevails! God says:

> *"Rather, We dash with truth upon falsehood and it shatters its brain, thereupon it departs, and woe to you for the falsehood you ascribe."* – **Qur'an 21:18**

God has given every generation of mankind a righteous and infallible role model with a perfect character to strive for and follow. As we have seen earlier, Prophet Mohamad was ordered by God to appoint successors from his progeny called *imams*; leaders to represent God and protect the sacred message from corruption. We saw that this lineage begins with his daughter Fatima, a.k.a. *Al-Zahraa* (The Rose), and his son in law Ali, son of Abi Taleb, a.k.a. *Ameer Al-Mu'meneen* (Commander of the Faithful). Fatima and Ali had two sons named Al Hassan, a.k.a. *Al-Mojtaba* (The Chosen One), and Al Hussein, a.k.a. *Al-Shaheed* (The Martyr). And finally, we saw that from Al-Hussein came nine descendants, each of them the *imam* of his time. Today, we have the twelfth imam, Mohamad, son of Al-Askari, a.k.a. *Al-Mahdi* (The Guided One), currently in occultation. Al-Mahdi is the final of twelve imams from the progeny of the prophet. All of them are the godly appointed representatives, protectors, and ambassadors of truth. I present to you the twelve imams again. This time, with more detail:

1st Imam: **Ali**, son of Abi Taleb
Also known as: **Ameer Al-Mu'meneen** (Commander of the Faithful)

2nd Imam: **Al-Hassan**, son of Ali *Ameer Al-Mu'meneen*
Also known as: **Al-Mujtaba** (The Chosen One)

3rd Imam: **Al-Hussein**, son of Ali *Ameer Al-Mu'meneen*
Also known as: **Al-Shaheed** (The Martyr)

4th Imam: **Ali**, son of Al-Hussein *Al-Shaheed*
Also known as: **Zeinul'abedeen** (Adornment of the Pious)

5th Imam: **Mohamad**, son of Ali *Zeinul'abedeen*

Also known as: **Al Baqer** (The Knowledgeable)

6th Imam: **Jafar**, son of Mohamad *Al-Baqer*

Also known as: **Al Sadeq** (The Truthful)

7th Imam: **Moussa**, son of *Al-Sadeq*

Also known as: **Al-Qadem** (The Serene)

8th Imam: **Ali**, son of *Al-Qadem*

Also known as: **Al-Reda** (Contentment)

9th Imam: **Mohamad**, son of *Al-Reda*

Also known as: **Al-Jawad** (The Generous)

10th Imam: **Ali**, son of *Al-Jawad*

Also known as: **Al-Hadi** (The Guide)

11th Imam: **Al-Hassan**, son of *Al-Hadi*

Also known as: **Al-Askari** (from the city of Askar, i.e., "The Askarian")

12th Imam: **Mohamad**, son of *Al-Askari*

Also known as: **Al-Mahdi** (The Guided One)

Collectively, along with the prophet and his daughter Fatima, these holy personalities are known as *AhlulBayt* (Members of the House).

Allah says concerning them:

Qur'an chapter 33, verse 33

"...Allah intends to remove impurity from you, members of the house, and purify you with utmost purification."

And chapter 42, verse 23

"...Say [O Muhammad], 'I do not ask of you, for the message, any payment except love for my kinship.'"

All of them are of a perfect character and Godly conduct. Although they never received any education from any other person in this world, all of them – including the holy prophet and his beloved daughter Fatima – have given humanity an abundance of knowledge and wisdom that never ceases to enlighten the world with the truth about God, human life, the multiverse, and the hereafter. Eleven of these twelve divinely appointed Imams lived as the perfect models of pristine purity in human behavior. They lived as exemplars of ultimate submission to God's will, but all of them were oppressed and martyred. Therefore, the twelfth imam, Al-Mahdi, was ordered by God to enter into an occultation, protecting him from harm until an appointed day. Only then will Al-Mahdi reveal himself, restoring order and natural harmony to this world, after it had been filled with oppression and deception. These twelve sacred imams had been mentioned in the previous scriptures sent by God, and we can see traces of this even in the current Christian bible. Indeed, the promise of the Lord to create *twelve princes* in the seed of Prophet *Ismaeel*, was fulfilled with God establishing the Twelve Imams as the progeny of the Holy Prophet Mohamad. They are the chosen ones from Ismaeel, prophesized as follows:

Genesis 17:20
"And as for Ishmael, I have heard thee: Behold, I have blessed him, and will make him fruitful, and will multiply him exceedingly; **twelve princes shall he beget**, *and I will make him a great nation."*

They are the fountainheads of the religion, appointed by God through Prophet Mohamad to provide guidance whenever there are questions or doubts. Hence, safeguarding the truth. For example, as was mentioned earlier, some Qur'anic verses dealing with war and violence have been taken out of context by people seeking to taint the religion of Islam. However, thanks to the interpretations and clarifications of the AhlulBayt, we know that these verses had been revealed in very specific contexts addressing the oppression present at the time. As explained earlier, the poor and the weak were being mistreated by the rich and the strong, and slavery was mainstream. The holy prophet fought this corruption, becoming the target of many raids, offensive onslaughts, treason and violation of treaties, as well as very awful acts of aggression toward his followers. It was in these specific contexts that God revealed to Prophet Mohamad the permission for defensive action and preemptive measures. Many people, however – even at the time of the prophet – have taken these clearly contextual Qur'anic verses out of their actual context, either as a result of ignorance, or a deliberate will to destroy the religion by ascribing evil attributes to it. If I were to present the constitution of the United States of America, and only said that it *"Deprives people of life… without due process of law,"* would I have done justice to the constitution? Of course not! Because, although they are indeed written in the constitution, I took these words out of context. As a further example, would it be fair for me to taint the image of a noble war general by calling him *evil*, simply because he ordered his soldiers to *"fire at will,"* and *"shoot to kill,"* without saying that he was defending his country against terrorists out to kill innocent people? It would be unfair because I took what he said out of the context he said it in. Likewise, it is very wrong to cherry-pick certain verses of the Qur'an, revealed by God to Prophet Mohamad under very specific circumstances, and interpret them outside of their actual context. Furthermore, whoever says *"I know the Qur'an,"* or *"I can interpret the Qur'an,*" would be lying because it is a book that encompasses realms far beyond human understanding. Therefore, the only persons capable of giving an accurate interpretation of this book, clarifying the meaning of its chapters and verses, are the ones that God appointed to do so, i.e., the AhlulBayt. No one else can claim to give an accurate interpretation of any of the verses contained therein. This is actually common sense. For example, who do you turn to when you want legal advice, or if you need interpretation on a particular contract clause? A random person walking down the street, a friend in law school, or an actual lawyer? Obviously an actual lawyer! The same becomes much truer for a book that continues to provide guidance to mankind after fourteen hundred years of its establishment. Hence, who is it that can interpret a book authored by almighty God? Certainly not a random person walking down the street, nor a person simply versed in its original language of Arabic.

Until today, many malevolent people use this form of treachery and deceit to deliberately taint the religion of Islam; they cherry-pick certain verses of the Qur'an and interpret them out of their context to sow discord, confusion, and hatred.

One example verse commonly used by these people is as follows:

> *"And when the sacred months have passed, then kill the idol-worshippers wherever you find them, and capture them, and besiege them, and sit in wait for them at every place of ambush..."* **– Qur'an 9:5**

A few days ago, I saw this verse mentioned as one of several arguments against Islam on a pamphlet left in a shopping cart. What is ridiculous is that not only was this verse mentioned on its own, deliberately removed from its context, but it was also incomplete. Here is how it was mentioned:

> *"Then kill the disbelievers wherever you find them!"*
> **– Qur'an, Surah 9**

Upon seeing this, I was at first upset... and then I smiled; I realized that these people are actually spreading this falsehood only to other ignorant people of no intelligence. Any intelligent person would ask the following questions before forming an opinion on the subject:

- Is this a correct translation and/or interpretation?
- What context was the verse revealed in?
- What do the preceding verses say?

- What do the verses that follow say?
- Why is this pamphlet here anyway?

The answers to these questions are as follows:

- *Is this a correct translation and/or interpretation?*
  No, because the verse is not speaking of *disbelievers*.
  It is speaking of a group of evil idol-worshipers from
  Quraysh, a tribe that enjoyed an elevated stature
  amongst the tribes of the Arabian Peninsula at the
  time.

- *What context was the verse revealed in?*
  This chapter of the Qur'an – as well as the one
  preceding it – was revealed at a time when the
  religion and its prophet were being threatened by a
  group of these idol-worshippers, who had broken the
  terms of an established treaty with the nation of
  Islam. The terms of this treaty were as follows:

  o Whoever wishes to become Muslim is free to
  do so.
  o Whoever wishes to be with Quraysh is also
  free to do so.

- No wars between the parties for 10 years.
- Muslims shall be able to return to Mecca for their pilgrimage in the following years.
- No assault on any tribe or on the parties involved in this treaty shall be tolerated, no matter the reasons.
- Muslims shall return anybody that came to them without permission from his or her guardian.
- Quraysh does not have to return any previously Muslim person wishing to join them.

After this treaty was signed, a tribe by the name of *Khuza'a* joined the Muslim nation, and a tribe by the name of *Bani-Bakr* joined Quraysh. As these two tribes had always been rivals, Bani-Bakr took advantage of the treaty between Quraysh and the Muslims and plotted to attack the Khuza'a tribe – they received support and armament from Quraysh. Their attack took place during the night as an ambush, whereby they killed 20 men from the Khuza'a tribe. The tribe of Khuza'a reported the massacre to Prophet Mohamad, who received revelations from God as to how to approach the situation. This led to a series of events, after which the prophet gave Quraysh 4 months to think about their ruthless subversion and repent. Otherwise, he would be forced to fight them in order to prevent any further oppression. As you will see in the preceding verses below, the prophet was commanded by God to actually continue the enactment of the treaty with those who did not contribute in any way to the attack, were not deficient toward the treaty, nor supported anyone of the aggressors.

- ***What do the preceding verses say?***

  It is first important to mention that out of the 114 chapters of the Qur'an, chapter 9 is the only one that starts **without** the saying, *"In the name of God, the compassionate, the merciful."* The reason is that the content of the chapter does not correspond to the compassion and mercy of God. It is a chapter in which God is angry and does not show mercy to senseless terrorists and corrupt evildoers. The preceding verses are as follows:

"A disassociation from Allah and His Messenger, to those with whom you made a treaty among the idol-worshippers. So travel freely throughout the land for four months, but know that you cannot cause failure to Allah, and that Allah will bring disgrace to the disbelievers. And an announcement from Allah and His Messenger to the people, on the day of the great pilgrimage, that Allah is disassociated from the idol-worshippers, and so is His Messenger. So if you repent, that is best for you. And if you turn away, then know that you will not cause failure to Allah. And give tidings of a painful punishment to those who disbelieve, except those with whom you made a treaty among the idol-worshippers, and have not been deficient toward you in anything, nor supported anyone against you, so complete for them their treaty until their term. Indeed, Allah loves the righteous. **And when the sacred months have passed, then kill the idol-worshippers wherever you find them, and capture them, and besiege them, and sit in wait for them at every place of ambush. But if they should repent, establish prayer, and give zakat, then set them free. Indeed, Allah is Forgiving and Merciful.***"*

- **What do the verses that follow say?**

"And if anyone of the idol-worshippers seeks your protection, then grant him protection, so that he may hear the words of Allah. Then deliver him to his place of safety. That is because they are a people who do not know. How can there be for the idol-worshippers a treaty with Allah and His Messenger, except for those with whom you made a treaty at Al-Masjed Al-Haram? So as long as they are upright toward you, be upright toward them. Indeed, Allah loves the righteous. How is it that when they plot against you and gain dominance over you, they do not observe any pact of kinship or covenant of protection? They satisfy you with their mouths, but their hearts refuse and most of them are defiantly disobedient. They purchased a low value with the signs of Allah and averted from His way. Indeed, what they were doing was wrong. They do not observe toward a believer any pact of kinship or covenant of protection. And it is they who are the transgressors. But if they repent, establish prayer, and give zakat, then they are your brothers in religion, and We detail the verses for a people who know. And if they break their oaths after their treaty,

and calumniate your religion, then fight the leaders of disbelief. For indeed, there are no oaths to them; [fight them that] *they may cease.*"

- ***Why is this pamphlet here anyway?***
  It is there because people have been conditioned to fear the religion of Islam. It is there because *so called Muslims* give the wrong image of Islam. It is there because human beings have become complacent to the twilight of falsehood. It is there because although the truth fears no question... silence still proliferates. It is there because Islam has been expropriated, annexed, and continues to be oppressed as the world teems with deceit. It is there because authenticity is obscured by a fog of disinformation. It is there because of hatred and bigotry, and Satan's fingerprint was found on the pamphlet.

In light of this explanation, the verse on the pamphlet no longer seems evil after all. On the contrary, it shows that Islam cares very much about fighting terrorism in order to provide a safer tomorrow for generations to come.

Because of this understanding, even a religious scholar should not interpret the Qur'an without referencing the interpretation of the AhlulBayt. In fact, God says:

> *"He is the one that brought down upon you the book. From it are decisive verses, they are the root of the book. And others are equivocal.* ***As for those that have a deviation in their hearts, they will pursue what is ambiguous of it, seeking discord, and seeking self-serving interpretations. And no one knows its interpretation except Allah and the ones that are firm in knowledge.*** *They say we believe in it, all of it is from our lord. And the only ones that remember are those who possess a core."* **– Qur'an 3:7**

I love this verse because it provides such a clear explanation of how to interpret, as well as how *not to interpret* the holy Qur'an. Again, the only persons capable of offering interpretations are the representatives that God himself has appointed with the authority to explain and clarify the meaning of the verses. Which brings me to another very important point: translations to other languages…

Many people have translated the Qur'an to the English language. However, one must understand that the Qur'an had been revealed in the Arabic language for specific reasons. Being one of the richest languages in the world, the Arabic language at the time of Prophet Mohamad was something that people prided themselves with. For example, they competed against each other by reciting poems that utilized very eloquent language structures. When the Qur'anic revelation began, people were astonished by its eloquence and very sophisticated use of the language, as well as its imposing structures that sounded out of this world (pun intended). Almost the entirety of the book not only rhymes, but also has a very distinctive and soothing rhythm that even non Arabic speaking people, upon listening to its recitation, find calming and reassuring. Because of these intricacies, any translation becomes basically the translator's interpretation of the verses. This issue has resulted in some translations completely changing the intended meaning of a lot of verses in the holy Qur'an. This is another reason why it was written in a specific language; to provide a reference to the ultimate word of God conserved in its pristine origin. Otherwise, the true meaning could have been lost in the myriad translations and interpretations, such as in the case of the Christian Bible. One of these appalling translations is pertaining to a verse in which God explains to men how to react if they suspect their wife to be cheating on them:

INCORRECT TRANSLATION of Qur'an, chapter 4, verse 34:

Men are responsible for women by what Allah has given one over the other, and by what they spend to provide (for the family). So the righteous women pray, and do not cheat on their husbands in their absence by what Allah has protected. And the ones that you are worried of their wrong doings, preach to them and do not join with them in bed, **and beat them**…

I was horrified when reading this translation/interpretation. I find extremely narrow the view of a person that interprets the Arabic word used in this verse as: *to beat,* or: *to strike.* The reason is that, although the word does actually include these meanings, there are over a hundred other meanings to the same Arabic word! These meanings include honey, heartbeat, increasing pain, shiver, swimming, strength, depth, peeled, mixed, contracted, rang the bell, fell asleep, ignored, embarrassed, cried, stung, stamped, appointed, mentioned, participated, quit the job, gave an example etc. In perspective of all these meanings, we realize that the interpretation should be based on the teachings of the AhlulBayt, such as what the prophet preached to the people that beat their wives. He told them, *"How could you hit your wife? And you do this with the same arms that hug her?"* Furthermore, what is also imperative for any interpreter to do is to reference the interpretation of *those that are firm in knowledge.* In the case of *"beat them"*, we can clearly see that the translator did not fully understand the meaning before attempting a translation, because the **correct interpretation based on the explanation of Imam Al-Sadeq** is actually as follows:

> *"Men are responsible for women by what Allah has given one over the other, and by what they spend to provide* [for the family]. *So the righteous women pray, and do not cheat on their husbands in their absence by what Allah has protected. And the ones that you are worried of their wrong doings, preach to them and do not join with them in bed, and* **turn your back to them**... *"* – **Qur'an 4:34**

Big difference!

I will share with you another false interpretation. This one is very interesting because its correct translation portrays how many factors play a role in any attempt to interpret the word of God. Therefore, this will prove that not *anybody* can do it without guidance...

Some people allegedly say that Prophet Mohamad did not know the difference between Mariam (Mary), the mother of Jesus, and Miriam, the sister of Aaron and Moses, due of the following verses of the Qur'an:

"And she came to her people, holding him [the baby]. *They said: 'O Mary truly an unprecedented thing has thou brought. O **sister of Haroon**, your father was not a man of evil, nor thy mother a woman unchaste.' So she pointed to him* [the baby]..."

– Qur'an 19:27 – 29

Therefore, these people conclude that the Qur'an is not the word of God because Prophet Mohamad made a mistake, unable to differentiate between these two personalities. However, a person cannot form an opinion on something they do not understand, such as in this particular case the Arabic language, before making an impartial study of the subject at hand. For example, Why do these people not ask questions such as: *what does 'ya okhta Haroon' (O sister of Aaron) mean in Arabic?* Besides, before I even go any further in this rebuttal, and for the sake of providing another factor that one must consider, does it make sense that the man that changed the world, the man that knew and explained that space is expanding, the man that knew that the crystallization of water changes based on sound vibrations, the man that knew the intricacies of insects as small as spiders and bees, the man that knew and elaborated on the human embryo, the man that knew that pain receptors end on the skin – all at a time when today's technologies were nonexistent – and more importantly, the man that knew, explained, and elaborated on the history of mankind since the dawn of time itself, would not know the difference between two *Mariams* no less than one thousand three hundred years apart? One would have to betray common sense for that. Now, in the Arabic language, *"ya okhta Haroon"* is a respectful way of talking, labeling someone with a particularity of a people. For example, if I say, *"Eric, ya akha laarab" (Eric, O brother of Arabs)*, it means that I am including Eric in the *circle of Arabs* as a brother in this particularity, and does not mean that Eric is *literally* the brother of all Arabs. Another example is if I say, *"Julie, ya okhta al rijal" (Julie, O sister of men)*, I would be associating her with a particularity of men, such as their *physical strength* for example, and not that she is *literally* the sister of all men. With that mentioned, the explanation of the verses in question are as follows:

Qur'an (Mariam) 19:27

Arabic transliteration:

Fa atat behee qawmaha tahmelohoo. Qaloo ya Mariam laqad je'te shay'an fariyya.

English translation:

And she came to her people, holding him [the baby]. They said, *'O Mary, truly an unprecedented thing has thou brought.'*

Explanation:

They were saying, *how is it that you have brought this child into the world without a husband?!* Insinuating that the child is illegitimate! What is she to do? Can she tell them something along the lines of *well... I heard voices, carried a baby for nine months, and now I delivered it and brought it here?* Were they going to accept, or even listen to her story and understand? No! So they said the following...

Qur'an (Mariam) 19:28

Arabic transliteration:

Ya okhta Haroon, ma kana abouki imra'a saw'en, wa ma kanat oumouki baghiyya.

English translation:

"O sister of Aaron, your father was not a man of evil, nor thy mother a woman unchaste."

Explanation:

They were telling her: *you come from a noble family, of the priests of Bani-Isra'eel (children of Israel).* Because Moussa (Moses) and Haroon (Aaron) were the imams (leaders) of their tribe in *Bani-Isra'eel.* The concept of *Imaamat* (leadership) was a very important family tradition amongst Jews. As such, due to the situation at hand, they obviously referred to that concept saying: *O Mary, you come from a noble ancestry of being in the family of Haroon...* hence, *"okhta Haroon"* (sister of Aaron), *AND your father was a good man, AND your mother was a virtuous woman, how is it that you brought this child without a husband?!* What is she to do? Well, she pointed to the baby because she knew it was no ordinary child...

Qur'an (Mariam) 19:29

Arabic transliteration:

Fa ashaarat ileyh...

English translation:

So she pointed to him...

Explanation:

So she pointed to him – the baby – and he, by a miracle from God, spoke from his mother's arms. Note how the Qur'an glorifies Jesus, saying that even as a baby he spoke from the cradle as one of his many miracles. Sayed *Radiyyeddine Eben Tawoos* told *Abdul Rahman, the son of Mohamad Al Azdi Al Koufi (A noble man from the third century after the prophet)*, from the book *Ghareeb Al Qur'an*, with reference to *Magheera, the son of Shoba (Prophet Mohamad's companion),* that Magheera said, *"The prophet of God sent me to the people of the city of Najran (the people that presented the argument) to preach."*

They said, *"O Magheera, haven't you seen what Muslims read: 'ya okhta Haroon', and Haroon is the brother of Moussa? Between him and Jesus is a very long time span."*

Magheera said, *"I returned and told this to the prophet of God."*

The prophet said, *"Return and tell them that these people were referred to by the prophets and the righteous that came before them. Haroon was the leader of his people, full of prestige and magnificence. He had an elevated importance in Bani-Isra'eel. Hence, when speaking to Mariam, they referred to this concept in order to emphasize the gravity of the situation... as in: 'a baby without a husband, and you are from such a noble decent?'"*

As we can clearly see, whether or not Aaron had a sister named Miriam is actually irrelevant to the situation. Having a sister named Miriam would not change the facts mentioned above. But the charge still remains; even today, some people still attack Prophet Mohamad saying, *"The prophet of Islam did not know the difference between Mariam, the mother of Jesus, and Miriam, the sister of Aaron."* Which, as just seen, has always been a refuted argument.

The area of Najran, with its seventy villages, was located at the border of present day Western Saudi Arabia and Yemen. At the dawn of Islam, this area was the only region where people left paganism, converting to Christianity for many different reasons. Prophet Mohamad wrote letters to several kings and rulers of the world, inviting them to the religion of Islam, and amongst the intended recipients of this message was Najran's Bishop *Abu Haretha*. The content of the message was as follows:

"In the name of the Lord of Abraham, Isaac, and Jacob, from Mohamad, the messenger of God, to the Bishop and the people of Najran. If you revert to Islam, I shall thank for you Allah, the God of Abraham, Isaac, and Jacob. Furthermore, I invite you to the worship of God, in lieu of the worship of worshippers. And I invite you to a mandate from God, as opposed to a mandate from worshippers. And if you refuse, you have to pay a levy [this levy/tax was imposed on men because they lived in an Islamic state/government providing protection for them and their families, as well as excusing

them from military service. Indeed, the religion of Islam believes that no man should be forced to fight for a cause that he does not believe in. Hence, this minimal yearly payment would act as compensation to the government]. *If you also refuse to pay this levy, then I announce war against you* [because refusing to pay would impact the government's system, just as well as if people evaded paying their taxes in the times we live in today – they would end up in jail].

[Then, the prophet included in the message the following verse from the Qur'an]:

> *"Say: O People of the book, come to a word that is equitable between us and you - that we will not worship except Allah, and not associate anything with him, and not take one another as lords instead of Allah. But if they turn away, then say: Bear witness that we are Muslim."*

[Finally, he ended his message with the following words:]
"...and peace."

After receiving this message, Abu Haretha gathered a group of highly knowledgeable people with the task of making an informed decision about the prophethood of Mohamad. Some of these personalities were actually prominent religious scholars as well. One of them, known to be very noble and wise, responded saying, *"I have learned that God had promised Prophet Abraham that the lineage of Prophet Ismaeel would bring yet another prophet into the world"*.

Abu Haretha asked, *"How can we confirm that this prophesized prophet is indeed Mohamad?"*

So they decided to send a delegation to Medina in order to discuss with Prophet Mohamad, and search for signs that might prove the legitimacy of his prophethood. They chose sixty of the most knowledgeable and rational people of Najran, who were led by three of their bishops:

- *Abu Haretha* himself, *son of Alkama*, the greatest bishop of Najran, who was also the official representative of the Roman church in the area of *Hijaz*.

- *Abdul Maseeh*, the head of the delegation of Najran, who was known for his intellect, wit, and ingenuity.

- And finally, *Al-Ayham*, a highly respected elder of Najran.

Upon their arrival, Prophet Mohamad read to them passages of the Qur'an and explained to them saying, *"What denotes you as non-Muslims, amongst other reasons, is that you worship the cross, eat pig, and claim that God begot a son"*. They replied, *"The messiah is God because he raised the dead, informed us of that which is unseen, cured the sick and the blind, and created a bird from clay"*. Prophet Mohamad said, *"He is a servant of God, and he preached the word to Mary"*. One of them objected saying, *"The messiah is the son of God because he has no father"*. Here, Prophet Mohamad relayed, as God revealed to him the following verse of the Qur'an:

> *"Indeed, the similitude of Jesus to Allah is the same as that of Adam. He created him from dust, and said to him be, and he was."* – **Qur'an 3:59**

They said, *"You are only clarifying the reality of Jesus to us, which is something we will not confess to, nor approve of. So come, let us debate as to who is more worthy of the truth, asking for God to send his curse upon the nominated liars."* This debate would become known as *Mubahala* (the curse).

Once again, a verse of the Qur'an was revealed as an answer to their challenge:

> *"Then whoever argues with you about it after knowledge has come to you, say 'Come, let us call our sons and your sons, our women and your women, ourselves and yourselves, and then supplicate to invoke the curse of Allah upon the liars'"*

> **– Qur'an 3:61**

Hence, Prophet Mohamad agreed to the *Mubahala*, which would take place in a nearby desert on the outskirts of Medina. This debate would expose any lie about religious beliefs.

The heads of the communities of Najran, as well as their leaders and other prominent figures, discussed this event amongst each other. Some said, *"Look at Mohamad on the morrow, if he comes forth accompanied by his family, beware of debating him. But if he comes with his companions, then surely debate him because it would show that he has nothing."* Meaning: Prophet Mohamad showing up at the debate with a materialistic provision, alongside the leaders of his army for example, or his troops as an apparent power, would be evidence of his lack of truthfulness. But, on the other hand, Prophet Mohamad coming with his family, away from any materialistic manifestations and invoking God through them as prophets are known to have done, would instead prove his truthfulness. This is because he would have dared to expose not only himself, but also his dearest people, which would be a sign of utmost confidence in his message. The next day, the prophet appeared as though he was a blessed tree with four sprouting branches.

To everyone's surprise, Prophet Mohamad chose from the Muslims only four people; his family. These four personalities were none other than Imam Ali (son of Abi Taleb), his daughter Fatima Al-Zahraa (Imam Ali's wife), and their two sons Al-Hassan, and Al-Hussein. The confidence and conviction that these sacred personalities illustrated created a lasting impression on everyone present. He chose these amazing personalities for two reasons. The first of which is the fact that this is his family, which provides further proof that the prophet's intentions were purely God related and in complete resignation to his divine will. If it was otherwise, he would have undoubtedly chosen to bring along the elites of his community, or even well-known dignitaries. To this, the bishop of Najran said, *"O Christians, I am looking at faces that God could move mountains with. Do not debate, for I fear you will perish, and there would not remain any Christian on the face of the earth until the day of resurrection."* Upon seeing this luminous blessed tree and hearing the words of the Bishop, the entire delegation of Najran began to discuss amongst each other as to whether or not to debate. Their unanimous decision was to ask Prophet Mohamad not to proceed with the debate, and that they agree to pay the levy required yearly. In return, the Islamic government would provide them with protection to their families and wealth. The prophet accepted. And so it was decided; the Christians of Najran would enjoy a series of rights under the umbrella of the Islamic government.

$$* \sim * \sim * \sim * \sim * \sim * \sim * \sim * \sim *$$

The popular event of *Mubahala*, and that which has been revealed in it *Qur'anically*, are considered the greatest virtue supporting Shiites' theology throughout history. Let us reflect once more upon this verse in order to understand this truth:

> *"Then whoever argues with you about it after knowledge has come to you, say 'Come, let us call our sons and your sons, our women and your women, ourselves and yourselves, and then supplicate to invoke the curse of Allah upon the liars'"*

– Qur'an 3:61

The elocution of this verse establishes the capacity and stature of the eminent personalities whom Prophet Mohamad involved in such an important debate, and whom Shiites take as leaders. Who are *the sons* that this verse is referring to? Well, although Prophet Mohamad had no direct sons, the verse is nonetheless considering Al-Hassan and Al-Hussein as his. And who is the only woman whom the prophet took to this critical event? Again, although the verse says *our women* (in plural form), there was none other than his beloved daughter Fatima Al-Zahraa. Born five years after her father's prophethood, in an environment filled with purity and faith, Fatima was not raised in *any* house. She was raised in the house of a messenger of God. Her father taught her the knowledge he received from God; bestowing upon her his divine information. Even as a child, she shared with her father the harm that he experienced from others. Having lost her mother when she was only five years old, she found refuge with her father, the prophet, who became her only consolation. He gave her everything she needed; affection, tenderness, love, and respect. *"You're the apple of my eye,"* he often said to her, and he also felt consolation in her. She cared for her father with such tenderness that he also used to say, *"O Fatima, you are the mother of your father"*. She was seven years old at the time of her father's departure from Mecca to Medina.

At a young age, Fatima Al-Zahraa became reputed for her intellectual maturity and adult-like rationality. Hearing of these amazing qualities, as well as wishing for an alliance with the prophet of God, Muslim noblemen began asking for her hand in betrothal. However, after asking his daughter Fatima for her opinion, the prophet rejected these proposals with apologies, explaining that her fate was one that God would choose. Then came a request from Imam Ali, son of Abi Taleb… Fatima and her father accepted his offer not only because they saw in him total qualification suiting her exceptional qualities, but, more importantly, because it was decreed by God. Narrations state that Imam Ali sold his shield in order to pay for Fatima's dowry and prepare a house for his bride. Their humble house with modest furniture became very rich in good values and exemplar demeanor, as well as spirituality and faith in God. Therefore, Ali and Fatima became a very happy couple, living a life of affinity, harmony, love, and respect for one another. When Fatima passed away, Imam Ali spoke of their relationship saying, *"By God, I never angered her, nor did she ever anger me, and whenever I looked at her, all my worries and sadness would dissolve."* They helped each other out, creating a fruitful marriage. Imam Ali never shied away from landing a hand with chores around the house, and Fatima was the centerpiece of his life... the perfect wife.

Fatima's wisdom, piety, and loyalty, made Prophet Mohamad be attached to her. She had a special place in his heart. He loved his daughter so much. If he was to travel, he would make sure she was the last person he would say goodbye to. And upon his return, he would ask to see her first. Whenever he saw her, he would stand up reverently and kiss her hand. He used to say, *"Fatima is a part of me... whoever harms her has harmed me, and whoever harms me has angered God."*

Her unprecedented qualities showed clear proof of her elevated stature with God, becoming known by many names defining her infallible character and personality.

Fatima was to the prophet a perfect daughter, to Imam Ali a perfect wife, to her children a perfect mother, and to the rest of humanity a perfect role model, all at the same time. She carried with them their hardships and pains because she had such a pure understanding of cause and effect, as well as an unusually wonderful perspective on life and the hereafter. One day, her father came to her house and said that he felt weak and tired. She told him, *"I seek refuge for you with God from weakness"*. Notice how the prophet went to no one else except his beloved Fatima... his place of comfort and peace.

"O Fatima, bring something to cover me with," he said.

"I brought a cover," she said, *"had him lie down, covered him, and as I began to contemplate him, his face illuminated like a full moon on a perfect night..."*

* ~ * ~ * ~ * ~ * ~ * ~ * ~ * ~ *

A Perpetual Link

After the death of the holy prophet, certain people wanted to deprive Fatima Al-Zahraa's husband, Imam Ali, from his Godly right to rule as an appointed successor; they wanted the position for themselves – ironically, after having pledged allegiance to him. However, Imam Ali was commanded by God not to confront the aggressors, have patience, and wait, because a direct confrontation would have resulted in turmoil – *"I plan, you plan, and Allah is the best of planners,"* Imam Ali understood. Indeed, Fatima was the chosen candidate with the necessary attributes to dismantle this coup against the religion. She is the perpetual link between prophethood and the Imamate (the imams of AhlulBayt) because God is pleased when she is pleased, and he is angered when she is angered. Therefore, whoever harms her has harmed the prophet, and whoever harms the prophet is cursed by God, as mentioned in the Holy Qur'an... and the truth is brought to light. God not only dedicates an entire chapter in the Qur'an to Fatima, but also emphasizes in it her value as a gift to Prophet Mohamad. This is summarized in the smallest chapter of the Qur'an, comprised of only 3 verses:

> *"We have provided you with Al Kawthar* [Fatima], *so pray to your lord and give thanks, it is your enemy that does not beget."* – **Qur'an 108**

This enemy of Prophet Mohamad was a man by the name of *Alaas*, son of *Wa'el Al-Sahami*. He attacked the prophet, alleging that he does not beget. As in, *Mohamad will not have a son to carry his name*. So Allah replied, "[He is the one] *...that does not beget.*" Because Prophet Mohamad had Fatima. And when the prophet passed away, Fatima's house was breached in an attempt to subdue her husband Imam Ali. The attack left her with a broken rib and the loss of her unborn baby. Following this tragedy... she passed away. Hence, her sacrifice was a protection to the religion because it exposed the masks of the aggressors; their actions angered God as they harmed his prophet by harming his beloved daughter.

One would think, reading about her attributes and qualities, that Fatima Al-Zahraa lived to the age of at least fifty, sixty, or maybe even seventy years old. However, an astonishing fact is that Fatima, having accomplished such a perfect character with so many responsibilities, only lived to the young age of eighteen years old. On her death bed, her baby lost and suffering from a broken rib, she tells Imam Ali, *"Bury me at night. Wait until the eyes of the people have slept, and bury me alone... in the darkness of night."* Another hallowed personality... oppressed... wounded... martyred.

* ~ * ~ * ~ * ~ * ~ * ~ * ~ * ~ *

Exploring Infinity

Remember the *Mubahala* verse? And how it says *ourselves and yourselves*? It is confirming that Imam Ali, son of Abi Taleb, is the embodiment of prophethood. He is the reflection of the prophets and the message that the seal of them, Prophet Mohamad, came forth with. This is in light of the fact that there was none other than him present for *Mubahala* to represent *"ourselves"*. This is also reinforcing the fact that he was officially appointed by the prophet as his direct successor on a day known as *Ghadeer Khom*, which can be seen in many recorded scriptures, as well as in several passages of the Qur'an:

> *"...Today* [Ghadeer Khom], *I have completed for you your religion, and fulfilled upon you my blessing, and I am pleased with Islam as a religion..."* – **Qur'an 5:3**

And...

> *"It is decreed that your guide is Allah, and his messenger* [Mohamad], *and the ones that believe and give charity while bowing* [in worship to God, i.e., Imam Ali]. *"* – **Qur'an 5:55**

It was recorded that Imam Ali was the only man in the history of human beings to have given his ring as charity to a beggar while bowing in worship to God.

Indeed, the biography of the Commander of the Faithful, Imam Ali, is an eternal portrayal of glory and sublimity in which we see the principals of majesty, uprightness, and unique characteristics. This was a man who devoted every aspect of his life to almighty God. Thus, he became the embodiment of the message of Islam. Yes, Imam Ali was *the talking Qur'an*. He is not *just another figure in the history of mankind*, but a man that God himself has appointed for humanity as a role model with a perfect character and personality. He represents Islam with the best representations, and portrays the most precise practice of the religion. Imam Ali outpaced space and time, becoming the template on which life principles are based. In fact, regardless of what my mind recalls about this phenomenal man, it would be impossible for me to elaborate on his infinite personality with the finite ink in my *pen*. Therefore, considering that this book is about the search and restoration of the ultimate truth, I chose to translate for you, dear reader, one of his sermons called: *The Sermon of Intercession.* He provided this speech one week after the death of the prophet. As you will soon see, it is actually the apotheosis of knowledge, wisdom, and above all... Truth! This sermon dictates the essence of life, as well as the attitude one must have in order to reach that which human beings spend their lives searching for: happiness. Keep this book in an easy to reach place, and open it to this sermon every once in a while to remember how every human should act and react, no matter the situation. And if you are a non-Muslim reader, prepare to understand, ponder, and love. If life is only 10% what happens to us and the other 90% is how we react, then I guarantee that the eloquent advices, pure wisdom, deep knowledge, and extreme foresight of this amazing sermon will entice any sensible reader to learn more, and more – and more – about the peak of eloquence that is Imam Ali, *Commander of the Faithful*.

* ~ * ~ * ~ * ~ * ~ * ~ * ~ * ~ *

The Sermon of Intercession

By Imam Ali, son of Abi Taleb

Thank God for having forbidden illusions from attaining his existence, and having veiled the mind from imagining his self, so that it refrains from confusion and misconception, and resemblance and mistaken identity. He is the one that never varies in integrity, and his perfection is not divisible in segmenting numbers. He separated things not by debating their locations, and he took possession of them not by means of dissolution nor coherence. And he acknowledged their existence not with instruments with which knowledge can only be obtained, and between him and his knowledge is no other knowledge. If it is said that God has always been, it is because existence has always been. And if it said that God will always exist, it is because the concept of nothing has been negated. So glory is to him, and he is exalted from the sayings of those that worship other than him and elevate another God a high elevation.

I thank him with the thanksgiving that he is pleased with from his creations, and has obligated himself with its acceptance. And I bear witness that there is no God but Allah, alone with no partners. And I bear witness that Mohamad is his servant and messenger. Two declarations that elevate speech and multiply deeds. A balance they are absent from is light, and a balance they are a part of is weighty. And with them is success in heaven, and deliverance from fire, and the passing on the *Seraat* [a narrow passage in the hereafter leading to heaven and under which is hell]. And with these two declarations you will enter paradise, and with prayer you will receive mercy. So increase your prayers in praise for your prophet and his family. Indeed, Allah and his angels praise the prophet, O you who believe, praise him and offer your salutations.

I will ascribe to Islam attributes that no one before me has ascribed, and no one after me will ascribe except in this manner. Indeed, Islam is submission, and submission is certainty, and certainty is ratification, and ratification is confession, and confession is performance, and performance is action. A believer does not take his religion based on his opinion, and he instead receives it from his lord and takes it. A believer's deeds show certainty, and a hypocrite's deeds show doubtfulness, and a disbeliever's deeds show denial. So I swear by the one grasping my spirit, they did not know their position, so they assimilated the denial of the unbelievers and hypocrites with their malicious deeds.

O people, your religion… your religion… hold on to it. Do not let anyone fool you, nor move you away from it. A bad deed in it is better that a good deed outside of it. Because a bad deed in it could be forgiven, and a good deed outside of it is not accepted.

O people, there is no honor higher than Islam, and no glory has more glory than piety, and no wisdom offers more protection than devoutness, and no intersession is more effective than repentance, and no garment is more beautiful than good health, and no prevention is more impregnable than safety, and no treasure is more valuable than satisfaction, and no money will stop destitution more than contentment in subsistence, and whoever is satisfied with bare necessities will be content and will have correlated comfort, and will have reached fulfillment. The bitterness of this life is the sweetness of the afterlife, and the sweetness of this life is the bitterness of the afterlife. The best form of asceticism is in the concealment of being ascetic. Indeed, ambition is the key to fulfillment. And a monopoly is the mount of languishment. And backbiting is the effort of the incompetent. And stinginess, arrogance, and envy, are the reasons for indulging in sins. And evil encompasses hideous shame, and it is the reins that lead to all bad. And corruption leads to destruction. And piety is the president of morals. There are some that are infatuated if someone boasts about them. And there is futile greed for false hope. And there is a form of begging that leads to deprivation, and a trade that devolves into loss. Owning a position is the stance of men, and there are many minds that are held hostage to the desires of a commander. Whoever muddles in affairs without looking at consequences will be exposed to extreme calamities. If anyone hastily approaches people with what they hate, they will say about him what they do not know. And whoever follows people's wrongdoings will have donated to them his dignity. And the worst of necklaces is a necklace of sin, and the worst of sins to God, the praiseworthy and exalted, is the one that is disparaged by the sinner.

O people, there is no treasure more beneficial than knowledge. And no glory more superior than composure. And no lineage is more eloquent than good manners. And no agony is more painful than anger. And no beauty is more beautiful than wisdom. And no accompaniment is more evil than ignorance. And no wrongdoing is worse than lying. And no protection is more protective than silence. And nothing absent is closer than death, the rich will not escape it with their money, nor the poor with their destitution.

O people, whoever looks at his defects will be busy from looking at the defects of others. And whoever is satisfied with the sustenance that Allah has provided him with will not be saddened by what he missed. And whoever is pleased with the share that Allah has provided to him will not feel anguished by what others have. And whoever is weak in keeping his secrets will not have strength to keep others' secrets. Whoever treats others with injustice will be rewarded with it. And whoever retrieves the sword of injustice will be killed by it. And whoever digs a whole to fell his brother in will fall in it himself. And whoever destroys the veil of his brother exposes the defects of his home. And whoever forgets his blunders magnifies the stumbles of others. And whoever stultifies people will be insulted. And whoever is impressed by his opinion will be lost. And whoever considers his mind to be all he needs will flounder. And whoever is arrogant will be humiliated. And whoever mingles with intellectuals is revered, and whoever mingles with scoundrels is abased. And whoever holds more than he can carry will be disabled, and whoever penetrates into hardships drowns. And whoever lets his anger take over will not be safe from being broken. And whoever indulges in too much entertainment will be known as a fool, and whoever attacks the tides will drown. And whoever befriends in the way of Allah will be rewarded, and whoever befriends for this life will be deprived. And whoever enters the doors of wrongdoings will be accused. And whoever talks too much will increase his mistakes, and increasing his mistakes reduces his timidity, and reducing his timidity reduces his devoutness, and reducing his devoutness kills his heart, and whoever's heart dies will enter hell. Whoever has prolonged hope for this life will perform wrongdoings. And the fool is he who looks at the defects of others, rejects them, and then accepts them for himself. And the maladroit is he who belittles the person he is giving something to. And whoever becomes pessimistic will have become indignant with God. And whoever complains about a calamity will be complaining about his lord. And whoever approaches a wealthy person, humbling himself for his wealth, will have lost two thirds of his religion. And whoever reads the Quran and enters hell after death, is he who read the verses of God with mockery. And whoever's heart is deeply filled with love for this life will be dipped into 3 things: unending melancholy, cemented avarice, and unreachable hope.

O people, there is no wealth like wisdom, no poverty like ignorance, no inheritance like politeness, no beauty like lineage, and no clarity like consultation. The most honorable deed of the generous is omitting what he knows. And the best of deeds for the capable is controlling his anger.

O people, in a human being are ten qualities displayed by his tongue: a witness who speaks of his conscience, a ruler who clarifies the different forms of speech, a speaker who gives the answer, an intercessor who provides for the need, a describer through whom things become known, a commander who commands with benevolence, a preacher who prevents wrongdoings, a consolatory who soothes sorrows, the presence of someone who expunges grudges, and an elegant person who brings joy to the ears. Speak, and you will become known; a person is concealed under his tongue.

The tongue of a human being is the servant of his mind. The heart of the fool is in his mouth, and the tongue of the wise is in his heart.

O people, I have five advices to give that, if followed, will reward your efforts. Do not beg anyone except your lord. And do not be afraid except from your sin. And do not be ashamed, if you are asked about something you do not know, to say: *I don't know*. And do not be ashamed to learn something if you do not know it. The value of a person is in what they know. So speak knowledge and your worth will be shown. And have patience because patience is from faith as much as the head is from the body. And there is no benefit in a body without a head, just as there is no benefit in faith without patience.

O people, know that he who becomes bothered by someone saying fallacies about him is not wise. And he who is pleased with the praise of an ignorant is also unwise. People are the sons of their philanthropy, and the value of every human is in what they provide. It is in silence that you find prominence. And due logic establishes majesty. And equity increases connections. And favors magnifies values. And good manners multiplies production. And humbleness completes the blessing. And with the possibility of provisions, leadership is necessary. And a good reputation subdues the opponent. And having forbearance with a fool wins more allies.

And being benevolent and having composure grants the title of generous. And leaving what does not concern you will make you preferable. The first compensation for the forbearance of a clement person is that people will help him against an ignorant opponent. Prosperity in a foreign land is home, and poverty in the homeland is alienation. Wisdom has been compared to infallibility. And prestige has been compared to disappointment. And modesty has been compared to deprivation. And diligence has been compared to conscience. The heart is the book of vision. Controversy destroys opinion. If speech is shortened, truthfulness increases. And if the answer is given hastily, truthfulness disappears. And if capability is abundant, desire decreases. And if time becomes corrupted, the ignoble become masters. And if the cruel rule, the honorable are persecuted. The instrument for presidency is the breadth of the bosom. A generous person can be more sentimental than your kin. An Opportunity passes as fast as a cloud, so grasp good opportunities as much as possible – otherwise, it will dissolve into regret.

O people, there is no good in being silent on a judgement, just as there is no good to speaking ignorantly. Know, O people, that he who does not control his tongue regrets. And he who does not learn becomes ignorant. And he who does not control his anger will lose his temper. And he who does not prevent himself is not wise. And he who is not wise becomes puny. And he who becomes puny is not revered. And he who is not revered is rebuked. And the pious is saved. And he who gains money unethically will spend it improperly. And he who does not forsake when he is laudable, will forsake as he is abhorred. The generous has never used obscene language. The zealous has never committed adultery. And the calumniator did not obtain revenge, nor did he erase disgrace. And anytime someone jokes maliciously, Allah discharges part of his intellect. And for every time a person feels delighted by this world, he will gasp on the day of judgement. He who succumbs to the success of sin will not succeed. And a martyred combatant is not more rewarded than he who is capable but instead forgives, and the abstinent is ought to be from the angels. Allah will entrust intellect to a person, rescuing him with it one day. One coerced stone in the garden is a guarantee to the destruction of the abode. The wealthy is fatigued. And he who wins by evil means is defeated. And he who asks for eminence without the right to do so will be humiliated. And he who asks for guidance from other than those who possess it will go astray. And he who opposes truth clings to debility. And he who prolongs grief will be overcome with sadness. And he who combats the truth will be combated by the truth. And he who deceives Allah will be deceived by Allah. And he who becomes scholarly is regarded. And he who is arrogant is dispraised. And he who is not charitable will not be thanked. And he who stopped saying *I don't know,* will fall into dilemmas.

O people, better dead than abased. And better patient than apathetic. And the trial precedes the punishment. Subsistence is better than extravagance. Live with bare necessities and do not beg. And he who does not give while capable, will not receive while in need. True wealth and destitution will be revealed after the Day of Judgment. Every hustled person requests more time to achieve. And every person given more time will give excuses delaying achievement. Beware of taking your blessings for granted, as not everything lost can be regained. And your body in the grave is better than burying your vitality. And being blind is better than a surplus of gaze. If people saw their forthcoming demise and destiny, they would loathe hope and conceitedness. Be as benevolent as you can because, as you do, you become better than benevolence itself. And evade evil because he who performs evil acts becomes worse than evil itself. Bountifulness safeguards honor. And forbearance subdues the obscene. And forgiveness is the alms of victory. And disengagement is your compensation of whoever betrayed. And consultation is the eye of guidance. It is finest to leave foreboding. And days benefit experiences. And the mediator is the wing of the requester. Whoever magnifies small misfortunes, Allah, the praised and exalted, tries him with greater ones. And patience is the proponent of day and night. And grief is the accomplice of time. Deceit is more eloquent than intercession, and being devoted renders deception to be an alluring proposition. And being satisfied with one's fate shows compliance. What you bring forth in this life is for your own, and what you halt in it is for the enemy. Whenever a person reveals the favorable circumstances of their life, causing people to praise them, time keeps in store for that person a day of agony. And whenever two callings are in opposition to each other, one of them is false. Offering relief to a person in grief is the expiation of great sins. And abreaction of an anguished person, as well as being hospitable, are the best of generosities. And creating jobs, as well as broadcasting courtesy, is the best of excellence.

O people, be amazed in mankind; they see with lipid, speak with flesh, hear with bone, and breathe with an aperture. The most fascinating component has been attached to the arteries of the human, i.e., the heart, which houses the substances of wisdom, as well as the opposite: its antagonist. And if anger is suggested to the heart, it becomes exasperated. And if pleasure makes it content, it forgets to be cautious. And if fear consumes it, alertness pre-occupies it. And if the means become available, carelessness abducts it. And if a blessing is renewed for it, it is taken by pride. And if it gains wealth, solvency corrupts it. And if indigence bites it, burden engrosses it, and weeping exhausts it. And if afflicted by calamity, worry exposes it. And if hunger tires it, weakness cripples it. And with excessive fullness, gluttony sickens it. Hence, every negligence in it is harmful, and every excess in it is corruptive.

O people, whoever increases abandons. And whoever gains authority monopolizes. And whoever was hasty stumbles. And whoever diminishes becomes abased. And whoever is generous becomes dignified. And whoever's wealth increases presides. And whoever is often calm becomes noble. And whoever ponders upon God's grace becomes blessed. And whoever ponders upon the essence of God becomes a disbeliever. And whoever humiliates with something becomes afflicted with the same. And whoever increases the amount of something becomes known by it. And whoever is amazed with himself becomes ridiculed. And whoever seeks guidance from Allah receives grace. And whoever is negligent fails to be just. And whoever obeys a telltale loses his friends. And whoever is lazy becomes willing to attain things that are out of his reach, leaving behind the things that could have been beneficial to him. And whoever jokes a lot becomes belittled. And whoever laughs a lot loses his value. And whoever curtails in his work becomes afflicted with distress.

It is because of its insignificance that this life is the only place in which God is sinned against. And it is because this life is limited that God bestows of what he has only after having left it. And a person that does not share his wealth and his self with God is not needed by him. The speech of the wise is a cure if it is truthful, and an ailment if it is false. Negligence is the key to misery. And in carelessness and laziness deprivation is born, and devastation is produced. The lineage of someone becomes corrupted if he does not possess civility. The lineage of whoever slacks in his work will not help in hastening it. And whoever abases his morals will not be elevated by his lineage's honor. And whoever loses his manners will not benefit from the manners of his forefathers. Whoever puts himself in a position to be accused should not blame whoever thinks ill of him. And whoever safeguards his secret will be in possession of choice. And any conversation that exceeds two people becomes revealed, and if it does not need more people, then it is enough. The best of deeds is defending your honor with wealth. Whoever frequents the ignorant is not rational. The wisdom of he who refrains from intrusive speech will be recognized. He who frequents the ignorant should get ready for hearsay.

O people, if death could be purchased, it would be purchased by the evidently generous, as well as the cruel stingy. O people, hearts have witnesses that drive one's spirit away from the path of those that are careless, and the brilliant comprehension of admonitions calls one's spirit to be alert of danger. And hearts have desire intuitions, but the minds prevents and forbids. It is at the end of distress that relief is found. And it is at the tightening of the cord of hardship that ease is found. And with misfortune comes easiness. And affable knowledge is found in experiences. And from aspiration comes the retention of experiences. And learning a lesson is a cautious warning that drives to guidance. And lessons are abundant, yet recipients are scarce. For lessons have reached their peak, and learning from them has reached rock-bottom. It is sufficient to you, for your mind, to make clear the path of ignorance as opposed to guidance. And it is sufficient to you, from the affair of your religion, to know what you should not be ignorant of. And it is sufficient to you, for your refinement, to refrain from what you hate for others. And your duty towards your believing brother is just as his duty toward you. And whoever considers only his point of view has risked his self. Success is not with the lighter and quicker, and planning before an endeavor will prevent regret. And the loss of opportunity is a choke. Conforming to people in their [good] manners will save you from their plots. And discussing with scholars produces their benefits and gains their virtues. Whoever hosts different opinions will be aware of the locations of faults. And desire is the enemy of the mind. Whoever abstains from nosiness will have his opinion equilibrated. Whoever controls his desires will have perfected his magnanimity, and his outcome will be favorable. And whoever honors himself will have belittled his desires. And whoever fortifies his desires has protected his value. And whoever withholds his tongue will have gained the trust of his people, and acquired his requisite. Whoever fulfills the right of he who does not fulfill his right has made him his servant. And whoever is charitable, no matter how small the charity is, will be recompensed by God. Whoever doubts his other half should avoid arguments. It is in the change of one's livelihood and life circumstances that his character is revealed. And it is in the delusion of assumptions that life's term is interrupted. And days reveal the concealed intents. The twigs increase when the branches are soft, and whoever's companionship is pleasurable will have an increase of brothers. And whoever infringes upon his brothers will lose their loyalty. And whoever is known for his wisdom will be recognized with solemnity and prestige. And whoever undresses the robe of piety will have armored himself with a shield of disgrace. The esteem of the believer is his independence from people. And abstinence is the adornment of poverty. And thankfulness is the adornment of wealth. And patience is the adornment of calamity. And humbleness is the adornment of ancestry. And eloquence is the adornment of the tongue. And justice is the adornment of faith. And tranquility is the adornment of worship. And memory is the adornment of anecdote. And lowering one's wings [being humble] is the adornment of knowledge. And civility is the adornment of the mind. And being cheerful is the adornment of forbearance. And altruism is the adornment of asceticism. And the expenditure of effort is the adornment of the spirit. And a surplus of weeping is the adornment of fear. And abstinence is the adornment of contentment. And the forgoing of gibing a person with a previous favor is the adornment of grace. And submissiveness is the adornment of worship. And abandoning what does not concern you is the adornment of devoutness. And the most honorable of satisfactions is to forgo desires. And the greater wealth is to despair from what others have. And contentment is a wealth that never depletes. And money is the substance of desires. And patience is the cuirass of destitution. And stinginess is a sign of poverty. And greed is the robe of misery. And it is astonishing to see the heedlessness of wellbeing from enviers, as well as the heedlessness of good frequentation and preparedness for the hereafter, from those that process acumen. The loss of loved ones is an emigration. And a beneficial kinship is received through affection. And the generosity of the poor is better than the aridness of the wealthy. And a cheerful face is better than a frowning intimidator. And a beautiful reply is better than a long delay. And an advice is a sanctuary for whoever grasped its meaning. And whoever extrudes his anger has hastened his demise. And whoever releases his gaze increases his regret. And whoever overcomes his desires makes his wisdom evident. And the grouchy becomes a bore to his family. And the treasures of provision are found in the amplitude of good morals. Whoever does not request will not receive, and will be lead to corruption. And whoever requests something will either acquire it, or part of it. And whoever acquires becomes capable. And whoever is wise becomes independent. And time has made it imperative upon itself to thank the recipient. And it is rare to find someone who will rule justly whether you spread wickedness or virtue. And it is rare to find a persisting friendliness from kings and betrayers. And it is rare to have your aspiration fulfilled. And humbleness clothes you with grandeur. There are many that are spending the last days of their lives striding on sin. People will not see the shortcomings of he who is dressed by modesty. And he who befriends his opponent has revealed his own flaws and tormented his heart. And investigate the aim of dialogue, for he who investigates this aim will lighten his affair. And you are guided when you oppose your desires. And he who is aware of what days are made of will not be inattentive to aptitude. And he who mends opposition reaches his objective. And indeed, with every gulp and every repast is a choke. And many meals have been prevented because of one. It ill behooves man to trust in two characteristics: good health and wealth; for he could become sick if he was healthy, and he could become poor if he was wealthy. And you do not acquire a blessing except with the vanishing of another. And every need has aliment, every kernel a consumer, and you are death's consumption. And every person has two partners in his wealth: the inheritor and incidents. And the worst of canteens one prepares for the hereafter is animosity against people in this world.

Know, O people, that whoever walks on the face of the earth will end up in its belly. And the day and the night race in destroying lifetime. And he who remembers the length of the trip gets ready. And he who often mentions death will be satisfied with bare necessities. And a content spirit will help in attaining virtue and abstinence. And a generous spirit will make it easy to be charitable and helpful. And whoever realizes that his words are from his actions will reduce dialogue except in what concerns him. And if God had not aspired to be obeyed, it would have still been imperative to obey him in request of his mercy. And if God had not threatened against his disobedience, it would have still been imperative to thank him for his blessings by not committing sin. And if God had not established prohibitions, it would have still been imperative for the wise to abstain from them. The wise never cheats anyone asking for advice. The intercessor of the sinner is his confession, and his repentance is his apology. It is surprising to see those that are afraid of the punishment yet do not stop, and those that ask for recompense without repentance. Between you and exhortation is a veil made up of heedlessness. And a wise act generates enlightenment. Knowledge has severed the excuse of he who makes himself feeble. And carelessness is darkness, and ignorance is murkiness. And he who obtains an advice from another will be happy. There is no growth for he who severs family bonds, nor is there abundance for he who is dissolute. There are ten parts to health, nine of which are in silence except in the mentioning of God, and one is in abandoning the act of associating with fools. The head of knowledge is kindness, and its disease is infringement. And from the treasures of faith is to be patient through calamities. And from infallibility comes the refusal of sin. A surplus of visits generates boredom. And assurance before insight goes against determination. Egotism bedevils the mind. Do not despair a sinner, as he might become good in the end. And many have performed good deeds, impairing them toward the end of their lives, steering themselves to hell.

O people, speaking leniently is a segment of generosity. And being eloquent and the spreading of peace are segments of worship. Be cautious of the onslaught of the generous if he becomes depraved, and that of the mean if he becomes satisfied. It is sufficient that contentment provides acquisition, and evilness leads to annihilation, and good temperament provides bliss. Deception is the foundation of opprobrium. The greedy is always bonded to infamy. Whoever adjudicates himself is victorious, and whoever is heedless of such judgment loses. And whoever fears is safe. And whoever learns from lessons becomes enlightened. And whoever becomes enlightened comprehends. And whoever comprehends grasps. And whoever ponders learns. And whoever learns detaches. And whoever detaches is saved. And whoever abstains from appetencies becomes free. And whoever abstains from envy receives people's love. And whoever is hasty will receive rest. Your shame is concealed as long as you are enjoying wealth. And conceal the flaw of your brother that you know you have in you. And absolve the fault of your friend for a day when your enemy is upon you. And beware of gyp, for it is from the characteristics of the vile. And do not aspire for someone that has refrained from you. And do not trust in a person that is often bored, even if he was associated with you, because a person that is in deep darkness will not enjoy a quickly passing lightening. And it is not fair to adjudicate against confidence with doubt. And the worst of brothers is he who you cannot be yourself with, and have to have some form of artificiality in his presence. And the best of brothers is he whose sight elicits trust, and his absence grants you assurance and serenity toward him. And an envious friend is an ailment to harmony. Whoever becomes angry with a person that he cannot hurt, prolongs his agony and torments himself. Whoever fears his lord refrains from oppression. And whoever is inconsiderate with words reveals his profanity. And whoever does not know the difference between good and evil is as abased as a brute. Any calamity is small compared to the magnitude of destitution in the hereafter. Woe upon woe… for pretending only because you are full of disobedience and sin. Comfort is so close to weariness, and misery is so close to bliss. And there is no good in good after which there is hell *[meaning that it might look good to you but it's actually bad or evil]*. And there is no evil in evil after which there is heaven *[meaning that it might look bad to you but it's actually good. Therefore, heaven or hell should be what is considered in every deed]*. And every bliss less than heaven is worthless, and every calamity less than hell is welfare. Destitution is a calamity, and worse than destitution is a disease in the body, and worse than a disease in the body is a diseased heart. Wealth is a blessing, and better than wealth is a healthy body, and better than a healthy body is a devout heart. And when one corrects his conscience, he realizes the great sins. And purifying one's deed is greater than the deed itself. And purifying one's intention from corruption is greater than a prolonged struggle. Woe upon woe… had it not been for piety, I would have been the most cunning Arab. O people, it is upon you to be pious in what is unseen and revealed, and in speaking the truth whether content or angry, and in moderation whether wealthy or poor, and in justice on friend or foe, and in labor whether energetic or lazy, and in being pleased with God whether in hardship or comfort. Abstain from wishful thinking, because it dissipates the splendor of what you receive, and belittles the aptitudes of God for you, and establishes regret as the consequence of your fantasy. Blessed is he who devotes to God his knowledge and his deeds, his abhorrence and his love, his intake and his omission, his speech and his silence, his actions and his sayings. It is splendid for the worker to perform his due diligence, and have preparedness for fear of unemployment. He gives advice if asked, and is silent if left alone. His word is true, and his silence gives an answer without effort. And woe! All the woe, to whoever is afflicted with deprivation, desertion, and disobedience, accepting for himself what he rejected for others, and degrades others deeds while doing them himself. And a Muslim is not a Muslim until he becomes devout, and will never be devout until he becomes ascetic, and will never be ascetic until he becomes austere, and will never be austere until he becomes sensible, and there is no sensibility except in the apprehension of God, and doing for the hereafter.

O people! There was on earth two protections from the punishment of God, the praised and exalted, and one of them was removed, leaving you with the other, so hold on to it. The protection that was removed was the prophet of Allah, peace and blessings on him and his family. As for the other protection, it is the request for forgiveness. Allah the glorified and majestic said, *"Allah will not punish them while you* [Mohamad] *are amongst them, and Allah will not punish them while they seek forgiveness."* – **Qur'an 8:33**

* ~ * ~ * ~ * ~ * ~ * ~ * ~ * ~ *

Imam Ali is magnificent. He is the embodiment of elegance, greatness, splendor, and truth. He was the very first person to submit to the will of God and his final prophet. Being devoted, generous, gentle, helpful, and dutiful, he became known – amongst other names – as The Father of Orphans, Commander of Bees, and Commander of the Faithful. At the same time, he also had such bravery as to be the first to respond to Prophet Mohamad's call in the *battle of the trench*, and fight the famous fierce warrior *Amr, son of Abdul Wod,* when none dared to face him. He is the one that removed the door of Khaybar with his bare hands. He had such bravery as to sacrifice himself by sleeping in the prophet's bed in his stead, knowing that they were plotting his assassination. Indeed, he spent his entire life striving to promote justice in this world until he became known as *the talking Qur'an*. Countless lessons can be learned by The Commander of the Faithful, Ali, son of Abi Taleb. He teaches us how this world should be perceived, as well as how to prepare for the hereafter, by practicing the most beneficial human condition: *selflessness*. *"This life,"* Imam Ali says, *"...is just a bridge to get somewhere else"*. Imagine someone wanting to settle, building his house on a bridge. Why settle on the bridge when it is just a passage?

This is to say that we were not created for this world. Allah says:

> *"And hell was brought forth that day. On that day man will remember, and what good will remembrance be for him? He will say 'I wish I had prepared for my life.'"*

– Qur'an 89:23, 24

And we see here once more the precision of the holy Qur'an. Although it is a book which was written over a time span of 20 years, it is still – and will always be – the most sublime portrayal of utmost precision. Allah does not say *in my life*, but instead says, *for my life*. He is telling us that our real life begins after death, which is what Imam Ali clarifies; we are mere strangers on this little planet we call earth – foreigners who will eventually go home. Therefore, *"prepare for your life and do not delay,"* Imam Ali said. He added, *"Do for your life as if you'll live forever, and do for the hereafter as if you'll die tomorrow."* He also said, *"Aim to live in this world without allowing the world to live inside you. As when a boat sits on water it sails perfectly, but when the water enters it... it sinks."*

As you can see, Imam Ali wants us to do our best to excel, treat others with respect, promote justice, and help this life thrive in order to leave a better tomorrow for generations to come. He also wants us to leave anything we have no control over to our lord. This eminent Imam wants us to keep in perspective that this life is a passage; a bridge that we will one day finish crossing, leaving it behind, replaced by the ultimate settlement.

Human beings are merely exploring infinity and, in order to fully comprehend, we have to look into the absolute perfection that is Imam Ali, son of Abi Taleb.

His legacy began on a blessed day in the month of *Rajab*, in the *year of the elephant*. Pregnant and in pain, *Fatima*, the daughter of *Asad* and wife of *Abi Taleb*, entered the precincts of the *Kaaba* (house of God) in Mecca. She prayed to Allah saying, *"O my protector, ease my pain."* Suddenly, the wall of the *Kaaba* cracked open. As she stepped inside, the wall closed behind her by an unseen force. She stayed inside for three days and no one could open the front door. And so it was that Imam Ali, the youngest son of Abi Taleb, is the only person in the world to have been born inside the holy house of God, built by Prophet Abraham so many years before. Ever since, whether they love Imam Ali or not, people from all around the world circle around his birthplace as part of their pilgrimage. On the third day, his mother *Fatima* came out through the front door of the Kaaba. And who was waiting for her? Who was the first to hold the baby? Well, none other than the prophet of God Mohamad. And so began the amazing story of his life, which ended in assassination by the *kharejite* named *Ibn Muljam*, while in worship prostration to almighty God. The apotheosis of truth… martyred.

Much appreciation must be extended to all the lovers of this sublime personality. Not only Muslims, but also non-Muslims because the love of Imam Ali, son of Abi Taleb, proves the understanding of all the qualities that make a human being great. These people are *the truthful people of the world.* I congratulate those who ask for justice in the name of Imam Ali all around the planet.

"If you love me, prepare to have many enemies."

— **Imam Ali, son of Abi Taleb**

Karbala

A battle for Truth. The failure of falsehood.

Wisdom * Patience * Bravery * Honor

The character of Imam Ali left a prodigious effect on his two sons, Al-Hassan and Al-Hussein. They loved their father so much so that Al-Hussein once said, *"If I had one thousand sons, I would name them all Ali."* But as Imam Ali said, when you love *truth*, you must prepare to have many enemies. On his deathbed, after being fatally wounded, Imam Ali conferred the leadership of the nation to his thirty seven year old son *Al-Hassan*, at a time when the rein of the so called caliph *Muaweya, son of Abu Sufian*, had left the nation with fear, apprehension, and distress amongst the people. Having fought Imam Ali ferociously throughout his life, Muaweya was not only a fierce opponent, but a cunning one at that. He had went as far as to employ many agents with the sole purpose of defaming the AhlulBayt. This is what Al-Hassan was up against; a villain that would stop at nothing to spread falsehood and destroy the religion of Islam. The irony is that Muaweya actually portrayed himself as a devout Muslim – which is not the least unfamiliar to us in this day and age; terrorists calling themselves Muslims abound. Imam Al-Hassan knew very well that confronting this evil regime head on would most likely result in unfavorable circumstances for the people, as well as for the religion of Islam. Therefore, in order to prevent the bloodshed, as well as to expose the true nature of the deceitful Muaweya, he decided after a few days of consideration that he would forgo his Godly right to rule as an appointed successor, and make a peace treaty that would have certain conditions.

Knowing very well that Muaweya would no doubt breach the agreement in one way or another, he explained to his companions that this peace treaty would be what exposes Muaweya for all generations to come. The following lines were amongst the terms and conditions of the treaty:

- The people shall enjoy amnesty in lieu of persecution.
- Lovers of Imam Ali shall not be harmed.
- The cursing of Imam Ali on the pulpit after every Friday worship shall stop immediately.
- No successor shall succeed Muaweya upon his death.

The treaty was signed by both parties, and Al-Hassan and Al-Hussein moved from Kufa back to Medina.

In Medina, the sons of Ali were a fountain of knowledge about the existence and purpose of human beings. Their evening lectures gained so much popularity that people, from as far as Egypt and Yemen, traveled to see the Imams and gain knowledge from them. Years passed and pupils became scholars. Al-Hassan and Al-Hussein were, after all, God's representatives on earth. Meanwhile, Muaweya was plotting. His secret agents stalked, kidnapped, and killed innocent people only for being followers of AhlulBayt. The public treasury became Muaweya's governors' personal bank account, and freedom became a luxury. Indeed, Muaweya's men would do anything for money and fame, all while his wicked son *Yazid* was indulging in gambling, drinking, and women. But Muaweya had plans for his son. If he died, Yazid would have nothing, as the agreement states that Al-Hassan would take over as rightful ruler. Muaweya plotted... *If Al-Hassan died,* he thought to himself, *I would do as I pleased and no one could stop me.* He was able to have his agents get a hold of the Imam's wife and convince her to poison him. *"He will give you a large sum of money, and make you his son Yazid's wife,"* they told her. Sometimes, no matter how close people are to the truth, they are blinded by its blazing light because of their weak sense of *vision*, and they are instead subdued by the twilight of falsehood... she accepted their offer. A few days later, Imam Al-Hassan Al-Mojtaba fell very ill and passed away at forty seven years old; oppressed and martyred. Before breathing his last, he conferred the leadership of the nation to his beloved sibling Imam Al-Hussein, who was forty six at the time. And although he requested for his burial to be beside the shrine of his grandfather the prophet, and his brother Al-Hussein performed his due diligence to fulfill his request, Muaweya used military force to prevent the burial. He was buried somewhere else. If we exercise our transcendental perception; our *Baseerah*, we would understand the importance of this detail, and reach the epitome of moral judgement.

Without Imam Al-Hassan, Medina was not the same anymore. The Imam was such a valuable source of knowledge that people felt a big difference when he departed. He was dearly missed. His brother Al-Hussein, now the officially appointed third Imam of AhlulBayt, continued preaching and teaching Islam for several years. His followers grew and knowledge spread far and wide.

Now that Al-Hassan was out of the way, the coast seemed clear for Muaweya to establish his son as the new caliph. Working as hard as he could to appoint his son Yazid as successor, it was not as easy as he thought it would be. First and foremost, Islam does not allow for a monarchical system of government, and the people knew this very well. Even though Muaweya was able to alter some subtle aspects of the religion, promoting his son to the throne was too obvious a matter to be ignored by the people. Second, Yazid was known to be a drunkard and cowardly abhorrent pleasure seeking being. Wanting to rectify this, at least until his son is accepted by the people, Muaweya instructed him to deceive the masses by undergoing a pilgrimage to Mecca, boldly faking his repentance to God. This mental conditioning continued, and people were eventually deceived by the twilight of falsehood. At the age of seventy five, after having suffered from a severe illness, Muaweya met his demise. Yazid, then thirty years of age, used intimidation, coercion, bribery, and threats, in order to force people into accepting him as the new ruler. The people eventually gave in to this dictatorship because their lives and that of their loved ones were at stake. However, Imam Al-Hussein and his family and companions, whose representation of Islam is one of truth, knew that the secret to freedom is courage. *"It is better to die on your feet than live on your knees,"* he said, bluntly opposing Yazid's tyranny, unafraid of his intimidating military power.

We learn from Imam Al-Hussein that when we know our purpose and realize that this world is nothing but a system of trials, we can adjust our synaptic circuitry. This, in turn, alters our thoughts and inclinations. Hence, we shape our destiny. And by shaping our destiny, we know where we are going. And by knowing our destination, the trip toward it is traveled in anticipation and happiness. Allow me to repeat myself; when we shape our synapses, we become one with the creator:

> *"My servant, obey me and you will be like me.*
> *You will tell something to be… and it will be."*

Knowing who Al-Hussein was and fearing him, Yazid ordered his governor in Medina to threaten the imam with death if he refuses to swear allegiance to him. Al-Hussein simply ignored the threat and was preparing to travel to mecca with his family for the Hajj pilgrimage. Before leaving, Imam Al-Hussein went to visit his grandfather's shrine, in which he fell asleep as he continually wept. His grandfather, the prophet, appeared to him. Al-Hussein said, "*O grandfather I salute you. The land of Medina has become small for me. Tyrants from amongst the nation are after my blood, and I am leaving Medina... with a heavy heart.*"

Upon reaching Mecca, Al-Hussein started receiving hundreds of letters from the people of *Kufa*, a city in Iraq, inviting him to swear allegiance to him as their leader. They wanted to overthrow the evil regime of Yazid and put an end to his reign of terror. To ascertain the legitimacy of these letters, Imam Al-Hussein sent his cousin *Muslim,* son of his uncle *Aqeel*, brother of Imam Ali, as an emissary to Kufa. Meanwhile, Yazid dispatched his spies to attempt to assassinate Imam Al-Hussein in Mecca. When Al-Hussein was made aware that a network of spies was closing in on him, he feared for the sanctity of the Kaaba; he knew that Yazid had a complete disregard for Islam and would stop at nothing to fulfill his desires. Thus, the Imam and his family and companions left Mecca, heading toward Kufa to confront him. The Imam was hopeful of the help from the people who invited him. And so began their famous journey of over a thousand miles. One from which most of them would not return.

As the Imam's caravan came closer to Kufa, he received bad news concerning his cousin Muslim, son of Aqeel, having been captured and beheaded by the newly appointed governor of Kufa, *UbaidAllah, son of Ziad.* Saddened, the imam cried. He gathered his companions and said, *"I want you all to know that the people of Kufa have turned against us, and my cousin Muslim was captured and killed. Those of you who prefer to turn around and go home are free to do so and without any guilt."* This statement from Al-Hussein is a revolutionary one because of having been said at a time of universal deceit. Indeed, even today, the mainstream politician will lie and give false promises just to secure the votes he or she needs to be appointed. Al-Hussein, on the other hand, is the exemplar of truthfulness and reliability. He said the truth knowing that it would result in a decrease in the number of followers he had, at a time when even his life and that of those most dear to him was at risk. This is pure proof that the Imam was not after worldly desires. Fearing for their lives, some of the people left the caravan and returned to their families. The Imam continued toward Kufa accompanied by his wife, sister, and children, as well as seventy two of his loyal companions.

Before reaching Kufa, the Imam's caravan was intercepted by a troop of Yazid's army comprised of about a thousand men, and led by a man known as *Al-Hor Al-Reyahe.* This army blocked the

Imam's path; preventing him from advancing. Their mission was to take Al-Hussein to UbaidAllah, son of Ziad. But the enemy troops grew thirsty and requested from Al-Hussein to provide them with water from his reserves. Being the representative of God on earth, Al-Hussein's compassion and mercy is beyond imagination. Indeed, although prophet Mohamad had shared with him the prophecy of his assassination, informing him that he would die thirsty in a foreign land called *Karbala*, Al-Hussein not only gave his enemies water, but even went as far as to spray their horses to give them temporary relief from the scorching desert they were in. Al-Hor then proposed to Al-Hussein to head toward a village known as *Naynawa*, and the Imam found the proposition reasonable. As they reached the village, Al-Hor received a message from Yazid instructing him to prevent any further advancement or retreat. In defiance to his attempt to stop it, however, the caravan continued onward until it was blocked by another division of Yazid's army, at which point they were forced to stop. Upon realizing that the area they were now in was known as Karbala, located to the north of the Arabian Peninsula (central present day Iraq) by the Euphrates River, Al-Hussein requested from his companions to set up camp. Remembering his grandfather's prophecy, he knew that this was their final destination. The battle that would soon ensue, on a day known as *the day of Ashura'*, would be studied by the seekers of truth all around the world, and remembered for the rest of eternity.

The day before Ashura', after having laid siege to and prevented Imam Al-Hussein's camp from reaching the river for several days, Yazid's army closed in on them. The enemy's forces were comprised of approximately thirty thousand men in cavalry, infantry, and archers. Imam Al-Hussein and his family and companions (having been deprived of water) were thirsty. They especially feared for their young ones, including Al-Hussein's six month old baby. They requested for the battle to be delayed until the following day, to which the aggressors agreed. That evening, Imam Al-Hussein had another revolutionary act of not only patriotic companionship, but also steadfast leadership. He said to his companions, *"The enemy's interest is in none but me. You are not obliged to carry this burden. It is on me alone. Therefore, I urge you to escape. Leave, go back to your families and live your lives. The night will provide cover, and I will turn off the lights so that those of you who want to leave can do so without feeling guilty."* These subtle gestures are the reasons why Imam Al-Hussein is so illustrious. His heroism was remarkable to the point of taking the time to think about what is fair to his companions in such dire times, when he knew he was only one man against an army of thirty thousand or more. Take a moment to imagine the picture of him facing the army single-handedly. What word would describe it? Confidence? Responsibility? Bravery? Valor? I think that spoken language is actually too limited to portray the magnificence of Imam Al-Hussein's personality and character. Nonetheless, one word comes very close... TRUTH! Imam Al-Hussein not only constantly remembered that he is on trial for every input and output, but as Prophet Ayoub (Job) before him, he also knew that obeying God renders his potential unlimited, regardless of the tribulations he faced. At the forefront of his mind, he carried a responsibility to righteousness against wickedness, and shaped his synaptic activity and cognitive reactions accordingly; he soared above the highest clouds of the human intellect. His actions, to the seekers of truth, undeniably dissipate the fog of corruption.

The love that his family and companions had for him was so strong that, when the lights were turned back on, everyone was still there. They all declared, *"We would never leave you O Hussein. Even if we were burned, tortured, and killed a thousand times over, we would still never leave you! We either live with you, or die alongside you."* Again, words are too limited to describe this phenomenal portrayal of sincerity, loyalty, truthfulness, dependability, thoughtfulness, wisdom, consideration, reliability, friendship, unselfishness, honor, responsibility, trust, patience, courage, bravery, faith, love, and finally... TRUTH! During the night, the worship, prayers, and supplications of Al-Hussein's encampment sounded like the buzzing of bees. They were in complete harmony with their creator from dusk to dawn, offering their last thanksgiving while holding a vigil on the night before a battle they knew they would not survive.

On the day of Ashura', the plains of Karbala observed the perfect representations of all that is revered in human disposition. Al-Hor *(the free)* Al-Reyahe, for example, upon experiencing the beauty of Imam Al-Hussein, had a change of heart. However, having previously opposed and threatened the Imam, he became concerned and worried about Al-Hussein's reaction if he were to ask for forgiveness and permission to join his group instead. Seeing signs of uneasiness, his companion asked him, *"O Hor, what's the matter? Surely, a renowned warrior such as yourself is not afraid of a battle of certain victory for us?"* Showing what is best in human beings, i.e., our ability to exercise our transcendental perception, Al-Hor said, *"My spirit is deciding between heaven and hell. And by Allah, I will not choose anything over heaven!"* He kicked his horse and advanced swiftly toward the Imam's camp. As he threw himself at the Imam's feet asking for forgiveness, Imam Al-Hussein raised him up and said, *"You are forgiven. You are free, as your mother named you."* Al-Hor fought and died defending the Imam of his time. Before the fight, Imam Al-Hussein said, *"It is such that the pretender* [Yazid]*, son of the pretender* [Muaweya]*, has given us only two choices: either war or humiliation, and our humiliation is* *not an option! God refuses this for us, and his messenger and the believers. Such it is, that I'm marching with my family although outnumbered and have been deserted by those who could have helped."* Indeed, the men, women, and children in Imam Al-Hussein's encampment all ascended to the peak of sacrifice for the greater good; the truth. After having witnessed the martyrdom of all his sons and companions, Imam Al-Hussein was the last to enter the battle; one man, boldly advancing against an army of thirty thousand, *"I am Al-Hussein, son of Ali. I swear that I'll not be abased. I defend the family of my father and proceed on the religion of the prophet."* As he fought and killed a great number of the enemy, he saw a group of them advance toward his camp. Fearing for his family, his sister Zeinab, and his daughters, he valiantly said with honor and dignity, *"O followers of Abu Sufian, if you do not have a religion and do not fear the day of resurrection, then be free in your world and return to your lineage, **if** you were Arabs as you boast!"* They replied, *"What are you saying, O son of Fatima?"* He said, *"I'm saying that **I** am the one fighting you…"* reminding them of the fact that he brought along with him even his wife and their young ones, showing clear proof that he did not come for war. He continued, *"…and you are the ones fighting me, but the women should not be transgressed. So forbid your henchmen from the daughters of the messenger!"*

During his last moments, while leaning on his sword to try to get back up and continue to fight, the enemy surrounded him. After having been heavily wounded by swords and arrows, a poet's interpretation of Imam Al-Hussein's uttered words are as follows:

> *"My Lord, I am pleased when you are pleased, and none but you is worthy of worship. I left creation behind, heading toward you with love, and I have orphaned my children to see you. So if my love for you cuts me to pieces, my heart would still not lean to anything other than you."*

If the power of emotions can cause Dolores to die of a broken heart, and change the physiological aspects of the doctor in the hall, one can only imagine the precipitation of wisdom on our synapses when we finally fathom Al-Hussein's attraction to the oneness of God. He showed all of humanity what it means to be moving toward almighty God, so vigorously established on his track. His ultimate goal was God, and he humbly lowered his head to take one step at a time toward it.

Imam Al-Hussein's successful life is the result of a series of successful days – including his last. He is the portrayal of the attributes of unity. And his love for the light that illuminated from the dawn of eternity shows its effect reflecting on the structures of unicity, and creates a warmth in the heart of every person of truth. This fervor... will never subside.

"I learned from Al-Hussein how to be wronged and emerge victorious. I learned from Al-Hussein how to attain victory while being oppressed." – **Mahatma Gandhi**

* ~ * ~ * ~ * ~ * ~ * ~ * ~ * ~ *

A Sacred River

Imam Al Hassan paved the way to his beloved sibling. He was well aware of the tribulations awaiting his brother by the Euphrates river, on the soon to become very famous land of Karbala, located to the north of the country by the Euphrates River. Indeed, the land of Karbala became not only famous, but also an institute of philosophy and wisdom for faith, honor, valor, bravery, loyalty, sacrifice, patience, eloquence, fervor, vigor, glory, dignity, serenity, and above all... love.

This echo reverberates in the hearts of those that seek the truth, wanting to uphold it. Imam Al Hussein surrendered his all. He painfully accepted the worst of calamities with patience and an utmost, unmovable trust in almighty God. The events of Ashura' *(the ten days)* were prophesied in many passages of the Qur'an. For example:

> *"By the dawn* [Imam Al Mahdi]. *And the ten nights* [Ashura']. *And the duo* [Imam Ali and Fatima] *and the singular* [Prophet Mohamad]. *And the night when it passes* [the night before the tenth day]. *Is there in this an oath for the intellectual? Have you not considered how your lord*

dealt with Aad? Iram, which had lofty pillars. The likes of which had never been created in the lands. And Thamud, who carved out the rocks in the valley? And Pharaoh, owner of the stakes? Whom oppressed within the lands. And increased therein the corruption. So your lord poured upon them a scourge of punishment. Indeed, your lord is in observation. And as for man, when his lord tries him and bestows upon him, and sends upon him favors, he says: 'my lord has honored me'. But when he tries him and restricts his provision, he says: 'my lord has humiliated me'. No! Rather, you do not honor the orphan. Nor do you encourage each other to feed the poor. And you consume inheritance, devouring it all. And you love wealth with immense love. No! When the earth has been pounded, crumbled, and crushed, and your lord came with the angels, rank upon rank, and hell was brought forth that day. On that day, man will remember, and what good will remembrance be for him? He will say 'I wish I had prepared for my life'. So on that day, none will punish as His punishment. And none will bind as His binding. O reassured soul [Imam Al-Hussein], return to your Lord satisfied and pleasing. So enter amongst my servants. And enter paradise."

– Qur'an 89:1 – 30

The tragedy of Karbala is popular not only in the Qur'an, but also in many of the other religious scriptures around the world, also prophesized in the bible:

> *"For this is the day of the Lord God of hosts, a day of vengeance, that he may avenge him of his adversaries: and the sword shall devour, and it shall be satiate and made drunk with their blood: for the Lord God of hosts hath a sacrifice in the north country by the river Euphrates."*

– Jeremiah 46:10

Dear reader. If you do not know about the unique feats of Karbala, or are not well versed in their intricacies, I urge you to learn. In Karbala, one sees the victory of truth against falsehood; the victory of good against evil. But be careful. What saddens me is that if someone was to perform a simple online search about *Ashura'* today, they will find many awful fabrications that actually have nothing to do with Imam Al-Hussein, or the sacrifice he provided to save the religion of Islam. They will find many awfully false traditions such as, to name a few, the bloody *self-flagellations, the walking on fire,* and the *portrayal of oneself as a crawling dog* – all *in the name of Imam Al-Hussein.* Many of the information found online today concerning Ashura could not be further from the will of Al-Hussein. Indeed, although this brave Imam wants us to acquire respect, honor, and dignity, these fabrications ultimately give the wrong ideas and create an unfortunately false understanding of what he stood for. And although Imam Al-Hussein represents acumen, prowess, and insight, many of even his own followers fail to see the problem; Satan is working very hard to inject a stream of falsehood into this radiant fountain of knowledge and wisdom. Indeed, Satan's fingerprint was found on this crime scene as well. But the Imam of our time, the awaited one… is ever vigilant.

* ~ * ~ * ~ * ~ * ~ * ~ * ~ * ~ *

Mohamad Al-Mahdi

The awaited one

Authority * Duty * Responsibility * Care

The birth of the twelfth Imam, Al-Mahdi, signified the dawn of hope for the oppressed in this world. His father is Imam Al-Hassan Al-Askari, and his mother is *Lady Narjess*, who is from the lineage of Peter, the disciple of Jesus. Imam Al-Mahdi is the last of the Imams of AhlulBayt, and just as Prophet Jesus was prophesied in the Torah by Prophet Moses, and Prophet Mohamad prophesized in the bible by Prophet Jesus, Imam Al-Mahdi was also prophesized by Prophet Mohamad on several occasions. His name is also Mohamad, and he is known as *AbalQasem,* as was known Prophet Mohamad. Knowing about the prophesy of the birth of a man that would fill the world with justice and equality, the *Abbasid*'s evil government at the time had the house of Imam Al-Askari under heavy surveillance. They were closely monitoring the family's every move in order to discover any sign of Lady Narjess' pregnancy, or the eventual birth of the Imam. However, just as almighty God protected Prophet Moses by not showing any signs of pregnancy on his mother, he also protected Imam Al-Mahdi. Indeed, no one could tell that Lady Narjess was pregnant until it was time to give birth to the Imam of our time. His father, Imam Al-Askari, was poisoned by the Abassid government's leader when Al-Mahdi was only five years old. Until then, the Imam had hidden his son except from his close friends, whom he knew were trustworthy of the secret. The day that Imam Al-Askari passed away, his brother Jafar (a.k.a. *Jafar the liar*), Imam Al-Mahdi's uncle, falsely presented himself as the successor of the Imam. As Jafar approached to lead the prayer, the young five year old Imam Al-Mahdi appeared. He demanded from his uncle to step aside and began to lead the prayer as the rightfully appointed Imam of the time. When the prayer was completed, Imam Al-Mahdi was, once more, nowhere to be found. He had disappeared from the crowd. This event marked the beginning of the first occultation, known as *the short occultation*, which lasted 70 years. During this time, Imam Al-Mahdi had appointed a total of four representatives, in order for him to indirectly provide guidance to the people. Before passing away, the fourth representative announced that he would be the last. Upon his representative's death, Imam Al-Mahdi appeared one last time before his disappearance into what is known as *the long occultation*. This occultation is ongoing even today. Awaiting God's permission to reappear, Al-Mahdi patiently suffers the pains of the oppressed, abused, enslaved, exploited, and helpless. Currently only in contact with the deserving righteous, he awaits the appointed day on which he will reappear to fill the entire world with justice and equality, just as it was filled with oppression and corruption. By God's infinite mercy, the last of the ambassadors of truth is hidden away from preying eyes, protected by God almighty. He is nonetheless manifested to hopeful hearts.

A shining light in a world filled with glooming darkness.

A sign of love and care. To justice… an heir. A beacon of hope!

$$* \sim * \sim * \sim * \sim * \sim * \sim * \sim * \sim *$$

When all the pieces are put together and we see beyond what seems obvious to our senses by acknowledging our synaptic self... when we sink in the fact that every choice we make, no matter how small, will impact the world... when we expose all corrupted links by closing our eyes to the twilight of falsehood, and seek the blazing light with all our emotional intelligence... when we realize what was before the beginning, that nothing is nothing, and that faith is beyond proof... when we broadcast what is often undisclosed, recognize Prophet Mohamad as the truthful, and seek the guidance of AhlulBayt... we enter into the ripples of a reverberating echo originating from ultimate truth.

I would like to end with a sentence that I will not tell you directly. Instead, to make it more interesting, I am enticing you to look for it. Although the sentence is hidden, you have read each word without realizing it. How, you ask? Well, I have separated them from one another as part of other sentences. They are very easy to find, however, given that the first letter of each of these words is enormous. Look for each and put them together. This sentence inaugurates our lives, enlightens our path, propagates from our heart, and launches us into the ultimate truth.

And upon you... be peace.

* ~ * ~ * ~ * ~ * ~ * ~ * ~ * ~ *

"What is the truth?" Kumail, his companion, suddenly asked.

"What do you have to do with the truth?" Imam Ali replied.

Kumail said, *"Aren't I trustworthy of your secret?"*

Imam Ali said, *"Yes. What sprinkles on you... overflows from me."*

"Would a person like you disappoint a seeker?" Kumail insisted.

Imam Ali answered, as Kumail was continually asking for more:

"The disclosure of the majesty of glorification without indication."
    "Tell me more..."
"Elimination of illusion with the awareness of what is known."
    "Tell me more..."
"Uncovering the veil in overcoming the secret."
    "Tell me more..."
"Attracting the oneness for the attributes of unicity."

    "Tell me more..."

"A light that illuminated from the dawn of eternity, its effect reflecting on the structures of unicity."

In The Name Of God, The Compassionate, The Merciful

"Did We not expand for you [O Mohamad] your bosom?
And removed from you your burden, which had weighed
upon your back? And raised high for you your repute?
For indeed, with hardship is ease. Indeed, with hardship
is ease. So when you are freed [from your burden], rise
[for worship]... And long for your Lord."

— Qur'an 94

Until next time…

Made in the USA
Lexington, KY
05 February 2018